E mālama 'ia nā pono o ka 'āina e nā 'ōpio.

The traditions of the land
are perpetuated by its youth.

EXPLORATIONS!

Hoʻomākaʻikaʻi

Program Workbook

compiled by
Hoʻomākaʻikaʻi Staff

Kamehameha Schools Press
Honolulu
1995

KAMEHAMEHA SCHOOLS BERNICE PAUAHI BISHOP ESTATE

BOARD OF TRUSTEES
Richard S.H. Wong, Chairman
Oswald K. Stender, 1st Vice Chair
Lokelani Lindsey, 2nd Vice Chair
Gerard A. Jervis, Secretary
Henry H. Peters, Treasurer

ADMINISTRATION
Michael J. Chun, Ph.D., President
Fred Cachola, Director, Community Education Division
Sharlene Chun-Lum, Director, Summer Programs

Copyright © 1995 by
Kamehameha Schools Bernice Pauahi Bishop Estate
Previously published as *Hoʻomākaʻikaʻi: Explorations 1994*

All rights reserved. No part of this book may be reproduced
in any form or by any electronic or mechanical means,
including information storage and retrieval systems,
without permission in writing from the publisher,
except by a reviewer who may quote brief passages in a review.

Inquiries should be addressed to:
Kamehameha Schools Bernice Pauahi Bishop Estate
Media and Publications Department
1887 Makuakāne Street
Honolulu, Hawaiʻi 96817

Printed in the United States of America

ISBN: 0-87336-040-0

EXPLORATIONS!
Hoʻomākaʻikaʻi

Papa Kuhikuhi
Contents

ʻŌlelo Haʻi Mua/Preface vii
ʻŌlelo Hoʻākāka/Introduction 1
ʻŌlelo a ka Mea Hoʻoponopono/Editor's Introduction 3
Hoʻokūpono/To Behave Properly 5
Kamāliʻiwahine Bernice Pauahi Bishop:
    Kona ʻIke Nui a me Kona Hoʻolina/
    Princess Bernice Pauahi Bishop:
    Her Vision and Her Legacy 7
Nā Aliʻi o Hawaiʻi/Hawaiʻi's Royalty 13
Nā Hōʻailona Hawaiʻi/Symbols of Hawaiʻi 21
Nā Mele a me Nā Oli/The Songs and the Chants 31
Ka ʻŌlelo Hawaiʻi/The Hawaiian Language 55
Nā Hula/Hawaiian Dances 71
Nā Hana Noʻeau/Crafts 85
Nā Meakanu Hawaiʻi/Hawaiian Plants 105
Nā Kumu Waiwai O Ke Kai/Ocean Studies 125
Nā Huakaʻi Mākaʻikaʻi/Field Trips 143
Home Hoʻonaʻauao/Boarding Life 153
    Ka Palapalaʻāina O Ke Kula/Campus Map 160
    Nā Inoa Hale/Building Names 162

'Ōlelo Ha'i Mua
Preface

Explorations! Ho'omāka'ika'i is the Hawaiian studies workbook for the Ho'omāka'ika'i Program. *Ho'omāka'ika'i* translates as "to be taken on a visit" and signifies the exploration of Hawaiian culture that students in the program experience.

The program is for Hawaiian post-fifth-grade students who are not regular Kamehameha Schools students.

Each summer nearly eighteen hundred students enroll in one of the seven week-long boarding programs offered on Kamehameha Schools Kapālama Heights campus. Through classroom instruction, field trips and rehearsals for a culminating performance, participants improve their knowledge of Hawaiian dance, games, language and music and other aspects of culture.

This book is the primary text used by Ho'omāka'ika'i teachers and students. Others may also find it useful in educational settings outside of Kamehameha Schools or in the home.

Perpetuation of Hawaiian culture is a major goal of Kamehameha Schools. Through Ho'omāka'ika'i and other programs the Community Education Division provides opportunities to Hawai'i's youth, particularly those of Hawaiian ancestry, to learn more about the proud heritage and continuing traditions of the Hawaiian people.

Fred Cachola
Director
Community Education Division

ʻŌlelo Hoʻākāka

Introduction

"Hoʻomākaʻikaʻi: Explorations" is the best known and most popular of Kamehameha Schools' yearly summer programs. It attracts Hawaiian *kamaliʻi* (children) from all over Hawaiʻi, the continental United States and foreign countries. Since the summer of 1968, when Hoʻomākaʻikaʻi officially began, more than thirty-five thousand children have attended.

While at Hoʻomākaʻikaʻi *haumāna* (students) attend classes and live in dormitories on the Kamehameha Schools campus. For some of the 255 students who attend each week it is their first exposure to Hawaiian culture.

The current curriculum of Hoʻomākaʻikaʻi reflects the cumulative efforts of the many *kumu* (teachers) and *kūpuna* (elders) who have contributed to the program over the years. These include the late Dr. Donald D. Kilolani Mitchell and the late Hoʻoulu Richards; Nuʻulani Atkins, Nona Beamer, Fred Cachola, Kaipo Hale, Sarah Quick, Mahela Rosehill, John White and Julie Stewart Williams.

A typical Hoʻomākaʻikaʻi day includes morning Hawaiian studies classes and afternoon field trips. In the evening the *kamaliʻi* may enjoy swimming, music classes or group discussions and write postcards home. The culminating activity for each Hoʻomākaʻikaʻi session is the *hoʻolauleʻa* (celebration) held on Friday evening for the families and guests of the children.

Teachers, *kūpuna* and education students from college attend Hoʻomākaʻikaʻi as well. They come to learn more about Hawaiian culture. They, in turn, will teach others what they have learned. In this way Hoʻomākaʻikaʻi touches the lives of *kamaliʻi* everywhere.

E ola mau ka Hoʻomākaʻikaʻi! (Long live Explorations!)

Sharlene Chun-Lum
Director
Summer Programs

ʻŌlelo a ka Mea Hoʻoponopono
Editor's Introduction

In addition to the larger goals discussed elsewhere, this book will help readers understand and identify proper uses for certain Hawaiian words.

Hawaiian words used in the text, other than proper names and song titles, are identified through the use of *italic* type. Most Hawaiian words, like most words in English and other languages, can have more than one meaning depending on how and where they are used.

Within each chapter of this book, in most cases the first use of a Hawaiian word or phrase in the text is immediately followed by an English word or phrase in parentheses ( ). This word or phrase shows the meaning of the preceding Hawaiian word or phrase as used in that specific situation.

In some cases, especially in musical lyrics, translations appear alongside, following or are left for discussion with your instructor.

Through your reading and use of these Hawaiian words you will come to recognize and understand them as they are used in this book.

Within chapters beginning with *Ka ʻŌlelo Hawaiʻi* (The Hawaiian Language) you will find occasional English words or phrases (other than song titles) set in **boldface** type. When these occur they are used to highlight English words for which you have earlier been shown Hawaiian equivalents. When you find the boldface word or phrase try to remember or look up the matching Hawaiian word or phrase.

E ʻoliʻoli! (Enjoy!)

Henry Bennett
Editor

Ho'okūpono
To Behave Properly

People of every culture identify certain practices and behaviors they believe correct and proper. These practices and behaviors are built upon a foundation of values. A behavior is an action which is observable and a value is a quality considered desirable. Some values may be special and unique to a specific culture while others may be more universal and common to many cultures.

The theme of this Ho'omāka'ika'i Program is *"ho'okūpono,"* literally translated as "to behave honestly or properly." Hawaiians of old recognized the importance of *ho'okūpono* (proper behavior) because it helped maintain *lōkahi* (harmony) and strengthen *'ohana* (extended family) relationships.

Examples of *ho'okūpono* include: *hō'ihi* (respect), *mālama* (caring for one another and the environment) and *ho'oponopono* (openly discussing family problems and asking forgiveness).

While at Ho'omāka'ika'i you will learn the value of these behaviors. You will also come to recognize such other traditional Hawaiian values, still important today, as: *na'auao* (wisdom), *'onipa'a* (firmness) and *aloha* (love).

We hope that by the time you leave Ho'omāka'ika'i you will have come to treasure the concept of *ho'okūpono* and continue to live it throughout your life, appreciating its significance to Hawaiian culture.

Kamāli'iwahine Bernice Pauahi Bishop: Kona 'Ike Nui a me Kona Ho'oilina

Princess Bernice Pauahi Bishop:
Her Vision and Her Legacy

Birth of a Princess

Princess Bernice Pauahi Pākī was born in Honolulu on December 19, 1831. She was the only child of High Chief Abner Pākī and High Chiefess Laura Konia.

Konia's mother was Luahine. Her father was Kaʻōleiokū, the first son of Kamehameha the Great. Konia, therefore, was Kamehameha's granddaughter. Pauahi was Kamehameha's great-granddaughter.

Soon after her birth, Pauahi became the *hānai* (adopted) child of High Chiefess Kīnaʻu and Governor Kekūanaoʻa. After Kīnaʻu died in 1839 Pauahi returned to live with her parents and hānai sister, Liliʻu, the future Queen Liliʻuokalani.

Pauahi's Genealogy

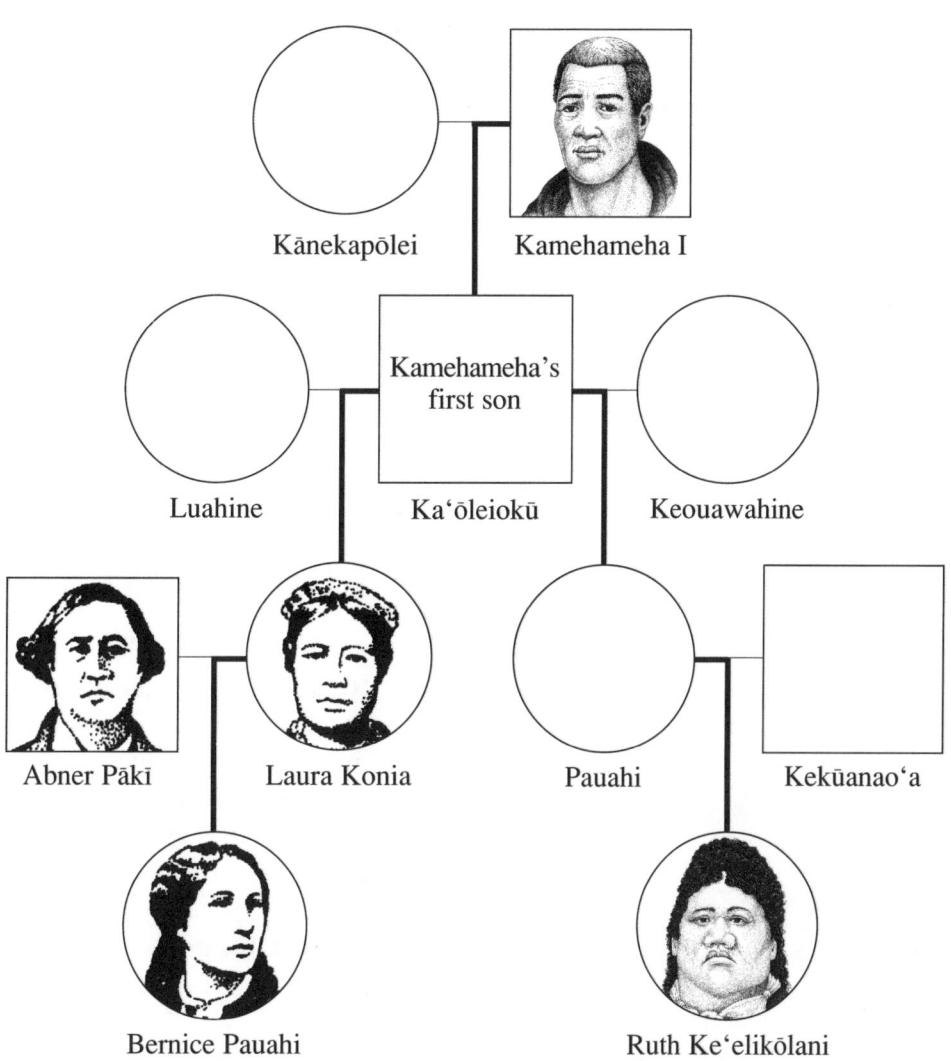

Legend

☐ male
◯ female

A School for Royal Children

At the age of eight Pauahi entered the Chiefs' Children's School, a boarding school for young *ali'i* (chiefs or rulers). Kamehameha III wanted the future rulers of Hawai'i to learn the English language and the ways of the foreigners. Christian missionaries Amos and Juliette Cooke were hired to teach the royal children. Their students included the five future monarchs: Alexander Liholiho, Lot Kapuāiwa, William Lunalilo, David Kalākaua and Lili'uokalani.

Pauahi became "the best educated of all the Hawaiian girls." She was "an interesting and brilliant conversationalist, ready to talk upon almost any topic." She loved music and played the piano and melodeon. She was very fond of children and often looked after the younger ones. It was she who taught the girls to play the piano and to sing. She loved the outdoors and horseback riding was her favorite sport.

Mrs. Cook described her favorite pupil, Miss Bernice, as "a most lovely girl—lovely in feature, form and disposition. Extremely prudent…is very fond of reading, likes history and is very well versed in it…plays and sings well, paints prettily, makes her own dresses, is now studying chemistry and Euclid.… I wish you could know her, you would love her.…"

photo courtesy of Bishop Museum

Marriage to Charles Reed Bishop

In 1847 American businessman Charles Reed Bishop visited the Royal School. There he met the young princess. The two fell deeply in love. They were married two and a half years later, on the evening of June 14, 1850, at the Royal School. Pauahi wore a gown of white muslin and a *pīkake lei* (garland or wreath of Arabian jasmine flowers). She was eighteen. Charles was twenty-eight. Pauahi's parents opposed the marriage and did not attend the wedding. They had hoped their daughter would marry Lot Kapuāiwa, the future Kamehameha V.

Of Service to All

After Pākī died in 1855 the Bishops moved into Haleakalā, the home of Pauahi's parents. Receptions, music recitals, piano lessons, reading, sewing sessions, meetings and tea parties were held at Haleakalā. The Bishops became the social and cultural leaders of Honolulu. Pauahi was a very gracious hostess and none were turned away.

The grounds of Haleakalā were full of beautiful trees, shrubs and flowers. Pauahi's favorites were roses and ferns. She enjoyed sending gifts of plants and flowers to friends and neighbors. She would gather flowers to take to someone who was ill and prepare a meal for that person. A tamarind tree planted on the property the day she was born was now quite big. Under this tree Pauahi counseled and comforted her people.

Pauahi brought together the best of the two cultures in which she was raised. She was a devout Christian and, as a true Hawaiian *aliʻi*, she served her people well.

Pauahi and her cousin Ruth Keʻelikōlani were like sisters. Pauahi was named after Ruth's mother. When Ruth became very ill in 1883 Pauahi took care of her and was with her when she died on May 24, 1883.

Aloha, Pauahi!

Pauahi was deeply saddened by Ruth's death. She was also very tired. Her health failed and she became ill with cancer. On October 16, 1884, Pauahi died. She was fifty-two years of age. Two weeks later she was laid to rest in the Kamehameha crypt at Maunaʻala.

Kamehameha V had offered the throne to Pauahi. But she turned it down. Perhaps it was just as well. The words of the Reverend J.A. Cruzan tell us why:

"The last and best of the Kamehamehas lies in her last long sleep. Refusing a crown, she lived that which she was—crowned. Refusing to rule her people, she did what was better, she served them, and in no way so grandly as by her example...."

Pauahi's Vision

As the last direct descendant of Kamehameha the Great, Pauahi inherited about three hundred fifty thousand acres of Kamehameha lands from Ruth Keʻelikōlani. Her parents and aunt ʻAkahi left her their lands as well. Altogether she had over four hundred thousand acres.

What was to become of her large estate? The Bishops loved children. Yet they had none of their own to inherit Pauahi's lands.

Pauahi's lands became the Bernice Pauahi Bishop Estate. Article 13 of her will directed the trustees of her estate to establish two schools, one for boys and one for girls, to be known as the Kamehameha Schools. Money earned from the use of her lands would pay for the education of her beneficiaries. She also directed her trustees "to provide first and chiefly a good education in the common English branches, and also instruction in morals and in such knowledge as may tend to make good and industrious men and women."

Pauahi's Legacy

Pauahi loved her people and her concern for them culminated in the founding of the schools which she named after her great-grandfather. Kamehameha Schools began in 1887 and has grown into an educational system serving students throughout Hawaiʻi. Each year its many programs, including Hoʻomākaʻikaʻi, reach more than forty thousand Hawaiians and non-Hawaiians of all ages. Truly, there is no end to the number of children that can be called the *hānai* sons and daughters of Bernice Pauahi and Charles Reed Bishop.

Nā Aliʻi o Hawaiʻi
Hawaiʻi's Royalty

The *aliʻi* (chiefs or rulers) played major roles in the traditional Hawaiian social system. They were leaders who used their authority to guide their people with wisdom and strength.

One of the best known and most powerful *aliʻi* from early Hawaiʻi was Kamehameha the Great. Recognized as the first *aliʻi* to unite all of the Hawaiian islands he is also remembered as a just and intelligent ruler.

Although the Hawaiian kingdom no longer exists the legacies of our *aliʻi* are not lost. Kamehameha the Great's "Law of the Splintered Paddle," our state motto *"Ua mau ke ea o ka ʻāina i ka pono"* (first spoken by Kamehameha III), Queen's Hospital (founded by Kamehameha IV and Queen Emma), ʻIolani Palace (built by Kalākaua), and Queen Liliʻuokalani's lovely song "Aloha ʻOe" all remind us of how the royalty of Hawaiʻi contributed immeasurably to the enrichment of the Hawaiian people. Their special gifts to their people will always be cherished.

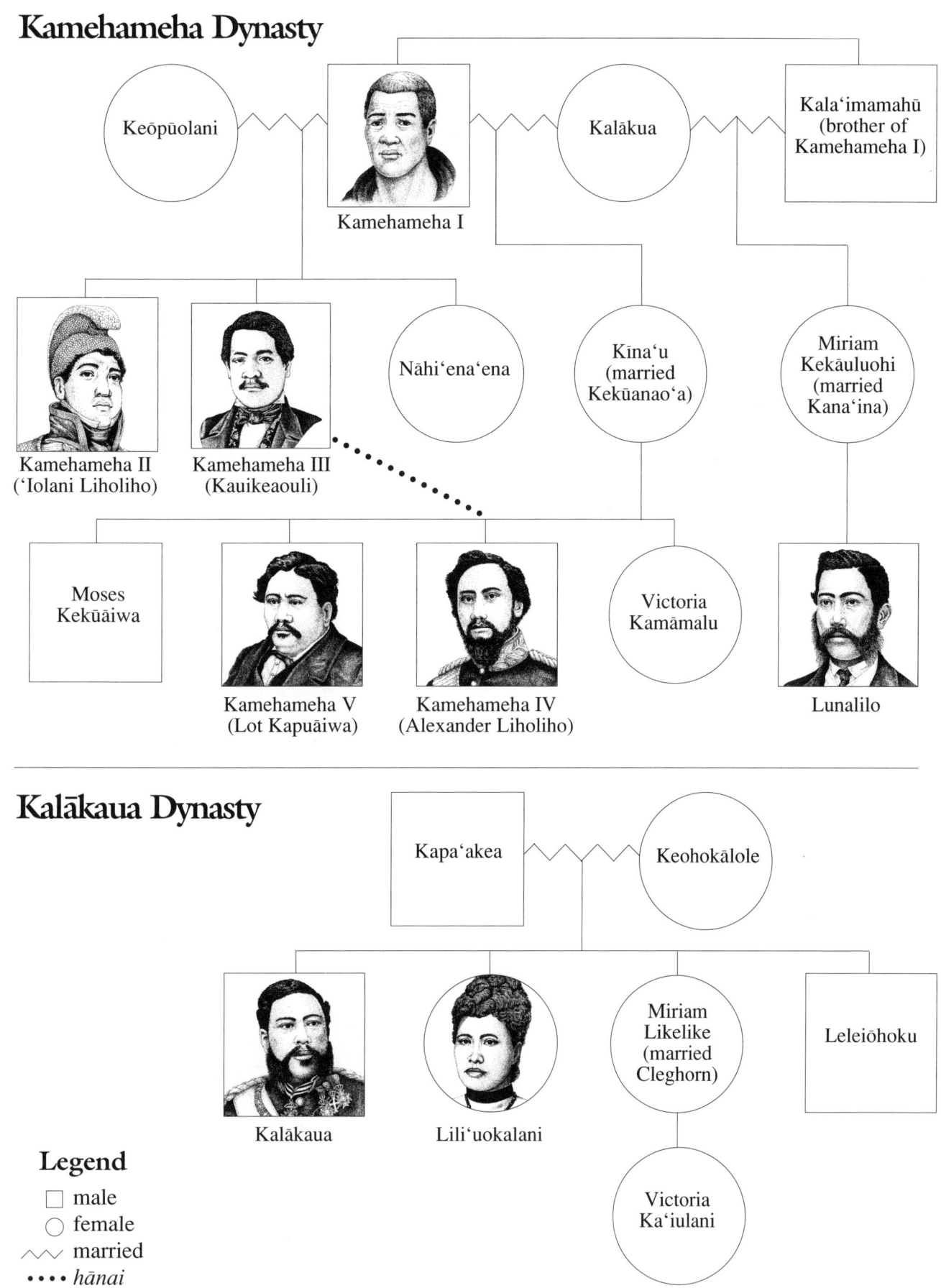

Kamehameha the Great (Kamehameha I)
1795–1819
- United all the islands

Kamehameha Schools
- Named for Kamehameha the Great by his great-granddaughter Princess Bernice Pauahi Bishop

Kamehameha II
1819–1824
- Co-ruled with Kaʻahumanu

Kamehameha III
1825–1854
- Spoke the words which became the motto of the state of Hawaiʻi

St. Andrew's Cathedral
- St. Andrew's Priory
- ʻIolani School

Kamehameha IV
1854–1863
- Helped to bring the Episcopalian religion to Hawaiʻi

Queen Emma
- Helped fund and establish Queen's Hospital

Ali'iōlani Hale
- Named for Kamehameha V
- State judiciary building

Kamehameha V
1863–1872
- Last great chief of the olden type

Kalākaua
1874–1891
- A renaissance man

'Iolani Palace
- Only royal palace in the United States
- The present building was built by Kalākaua in 1882 replacing an earlier structure of the same name

Lunalilo
1873–1874
- First king to be elected

Lunalilo's Tomb
- On Kawaiahaʻo Church grounds

Kawaiahaʻo Church
- 14,000 blocks of coral

'O Lili'uokalani

Lydia Kamaka'eha Lili'uokalani was the first and only queen to rule Hawai'i. She succeeded her older brother, King Kalākaua, on January 29, 1891.

Queen Lili'uokalani tried to restore the power of the monarchy but her efforts met with much opposition. To avoid bloodshed she stepped down from the throne peacefully on January 17, 1893.

In 1894 a plot to overthrow the government of the republic of Hawai'i and return the monarchy ended in failure. Queen Lili'uokalani was arrested and tried. Testimony at her trial failed to prove that she had any part in the plot. However the queen was found guilty of knowing of the plot and failing to report it. For this she was imprisoned in 'Iolani Palace for six months. To reduce the punishment for those actually involved in the plot the queen formally abdicated, or gave up her throne, on January 24, 1895, promising allegiance to the republic.

Lili'uokalani was educated at The Royal School (The Chiefs' Children's School). In her memoirs she wrote: "I was a studious girl, and the acquisition of knowledge has been a passion with me during my whole life."

The queen was an author, a musician and a composer. The songs for which she is best remembered are "The Queen's Prayer," written during her imprisonment, and "Aloha 'Oe."

Queen Lili'uokalani was the last of the royal rulers. On November 11, 1917, at the age of 79, she died at her home, Washington Place.

Washington Place
- Queen Lili'uokalani's home
- Now the governor's residence
- Lili'uokalani's personal belongings are preserved here

Nā Hōʻailona Hawaiʻi

Symbols of Hawaiʻi

Symbols—physical, visual or spoken—have always been an important element of Hawaiian society.

As Hawaiʻi entered the twentieth century certain images were selected to represent the islands. The Hawaiian flag (adapted from the British Union Jack), the royal coat of arms and the Great Seal of Hawaiʻi symbolize sovereignty. The *aloalo* (yellow hibiscus), *kukui* (candlenut) and *nēnē* (Hawaiian goose) all help portray Hawaiʻi's "from the mountains to the sea" environment.

These images exemplify the uniqueness of Hawaiʻi and help characterize all that is special about our wonderful home.

Ka Hae Hawai'i
The Hawaiian Flag

Ua mau ke ea o ka 'āina i ka pono
The life of the land is perpetuated in righteousness

This is the motto of the state of Hawai'i. It was first used in a speech given by Kamehameha III in July 1843 at Kawaiaha'o Church when Hawai'i's independence had been restored by the British.

The Royal Coat of Arms of the Kingdom of Hawai'i

The coat of arms of the kingdom of Hawai'i became an official symbol in May 1845. It was designed by Timothy Ha'alilio, private secretary to Kamehameha III. A feather cape was added to the initial design as a background for the central element. Additional changes were made while Kalākaua was king.

Arms
- First and fourth quarters: the eight stripes of the Hawaiian flag
- Center: ancient flag of Hawaiian chiefs with two spears crossed, an emblem of things or places or people *kapu* (forbidden or sacred) and under protection
- Second and third quarters: *pūlo'ulo'u*, a *kapa* (tapa) covered ball on a stick, another emblem of *kapu* protection

Supporters
- Two chiefs, facing inward, represent the twin warriors who supported Kamehameha I:
  Chief Kamanawa holds a spear and
  Chief Kame'eiamoku holds a *kāhili* (feather standard)

Crest
- Royal crown, ornamented with the *kalo* (taro) leaf

Motto
- "The life of the land is perpetuated in righteousness."

A coat of arms or a seal symbolizes the sovereignty or authority of a country. It is used by governments to authenticate important documents. It proves that those documents are trustworthy.

Hawai'i Pono'ī
State Song of Hawai'i

Hawai'i's own true sons

Be loyal to your chief

Your country's liege and lord

The *Ali'i*

Father above us all

Kamehameha *ē*

We shall defend

With spear

ali'i (chiefs or rulers)
ihe (spear)
Kamehameha I (the Great)—first king of all Hawai'i

Hawai'i Pono'ī
(Hawai'i's Own People)

lyrics: Kalākaua   music: Henry Berger

25

The Great Seal of the State of Hawai‘i

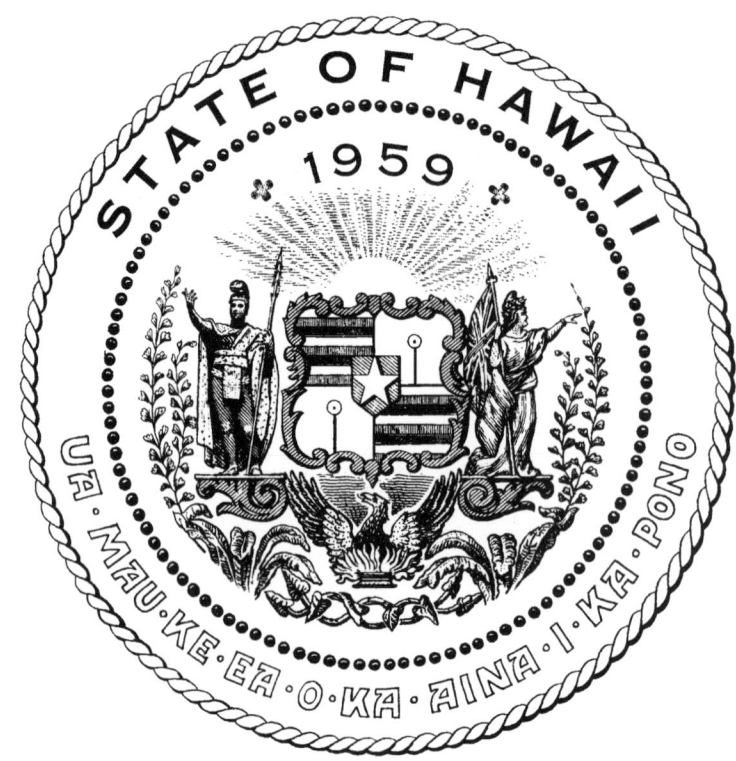

Viggo Jacobsen designed the first great seal in 1895 while Hawai‘i was a republic. Each part of the design has a special meaning.

Arms	• Eight stripes of the Hawaiian flag: eight islands • *Kapu* sticks: traditional emblem of *ali‘i* authority and protection • Star of Hawai‘i: Hawai‘i's star in the American flag
Supporters	• King Kamehameha I: the old era • Goddess of Liberty: the new era
Crest	• Rising sun: dawning of the new era • 1959: year of statehood
Motto	• "The life of the land is perpetuated in righteousness."
Further accessories	• Phoenix bird, rising from flames: a new Hawai‘i emerging • Eight *kalo* leaves: eight islands • Banana leaves: fruitfulness of Hawai‘i • Maidenhair fern: greenness of Hawai‘i

State Flower of Hawai'i

Aloalo

yellow hibiscus

State Tree of Hawai‘i

Kukui

candlenut

State Bird of Hawai‘i

Nēnē

Hawaiian goose

Nā Mele a me Nā Oli
The Songs and the Chants

Hawaiian music and poetry are similar. The poems are sung and the music grows from the words. The poems are word pictures which tell stories about the Hawaiians love for nature and people. Many different kinds of *mele* (songs) told the history of a family or honored a god or goddess or an *aliʻi* (chiefs or rulers).

One special kind of song was the *mele inoa* (name song). Many Hawaiians had a name song made just for them. The *mele inoa* for an *aliʻi* told about great things that had been done by the family and it also told of the great things the *aliʻi* might do later in life.

Some Hawaiian music was sung and some was chanted. The chants were called *oli*. They were chanted mostly in one tone. *Oli* had long lines or thoughts which the chanter had to finish in one breath. Sometimes he had to make his voice trill or flutter at the end of the line.

There were many songs for the *hula* (Hawaiian dance). These were called *mele hula*. Special chanters sang these *mele* while other people danced or the dancers themselves sang as they did the *hula*.

While attending Hoʻomākaʻikaʻi you will learn the words and melodies of graces and hymns, traditional songs, songs for plants and songs for the ocean. You will also learn songs poetically describing each island.

Hoʻomākaʻikaʻi

words and music: Mahela Rosehill

      Bb F   C7   F
Ei nei—look at us!
      Bb F   C7   F
Ei nei—look at us!
          G7   C7 F
Hoʻomākaʻikaʻi __

F
We are the youth of *Hawaiʻi nei*
                          F7
We are the chosen sons and daughters
Bb   F   C7
Who are bound together by rich traditions
                              F F7
That's us (clap, clap)—*Hoʻomākaʻikaʻi* ____
Bb   F C7   F F7
We play fair, we are alert!
Bb   F C7   F F7
We are not lazy, and we do not fear work!
Bb   F
We are strong in mind and body;
C7   F F7
We are strong in character.
Bb   F   C7
And we strive to gain wisdom,

For we are the youth (clap, clap),
              F
Of *Hoʻomākaʻikaʻi* ___

      Bb F   C7   F
Ei nei—look at us!
      Bb F   C7   F
Ei nei—look at us!
          G7   C7 F
Hoʻomākaʻikaʻi ___

Nā Mele o Nā Mokupuni
songs of the islands

Hawai'i

Waihoʻoluʻu: ʻUlaʻula *Pua:* ʻŌhiʻa lehua *Mele:* Hilo March

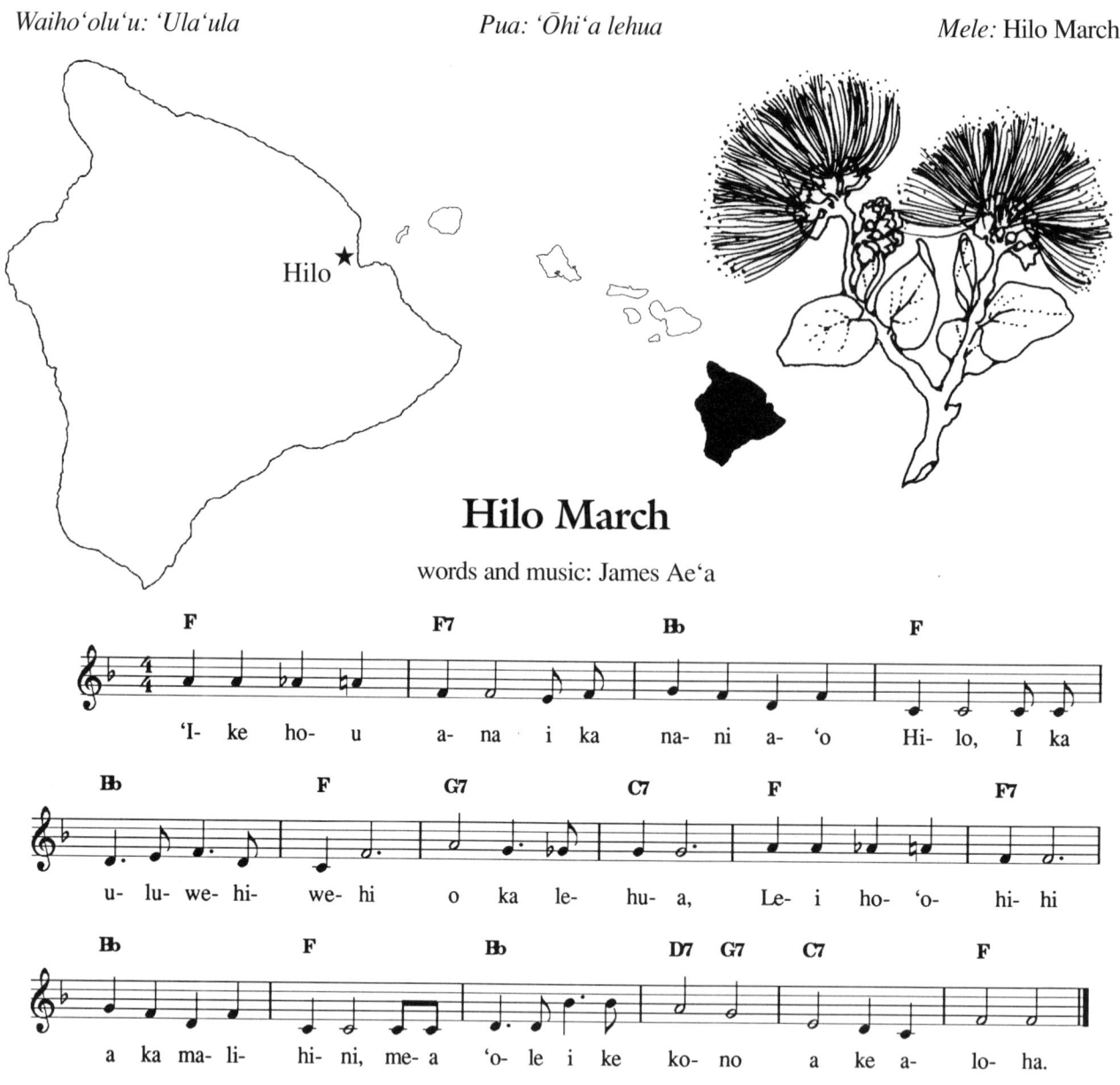

Hilo March

words and music: James Aeʻa

ʻI- ke ho- u a- na i ka na- ni a- ʻo Hi- lo, I ka
u- lu- we- hi- we- hi o ka le- hu- a, Le- i hoʻo- hi- hi
a ka ma- li- hi- ni, me a ʻo- le i ke ko- no a ke a- lo- ha.

We shall see again the beauty of Hilo,
The beautiful grove of *lehua*,
A *lei* much fancied by visitors,
Nothing deters the invitation of love.

Maui

Waihoʻoluʻu: ʻĀkala *Pua:* Lokelani *Mele:* Maui Nō Ka ʻOi

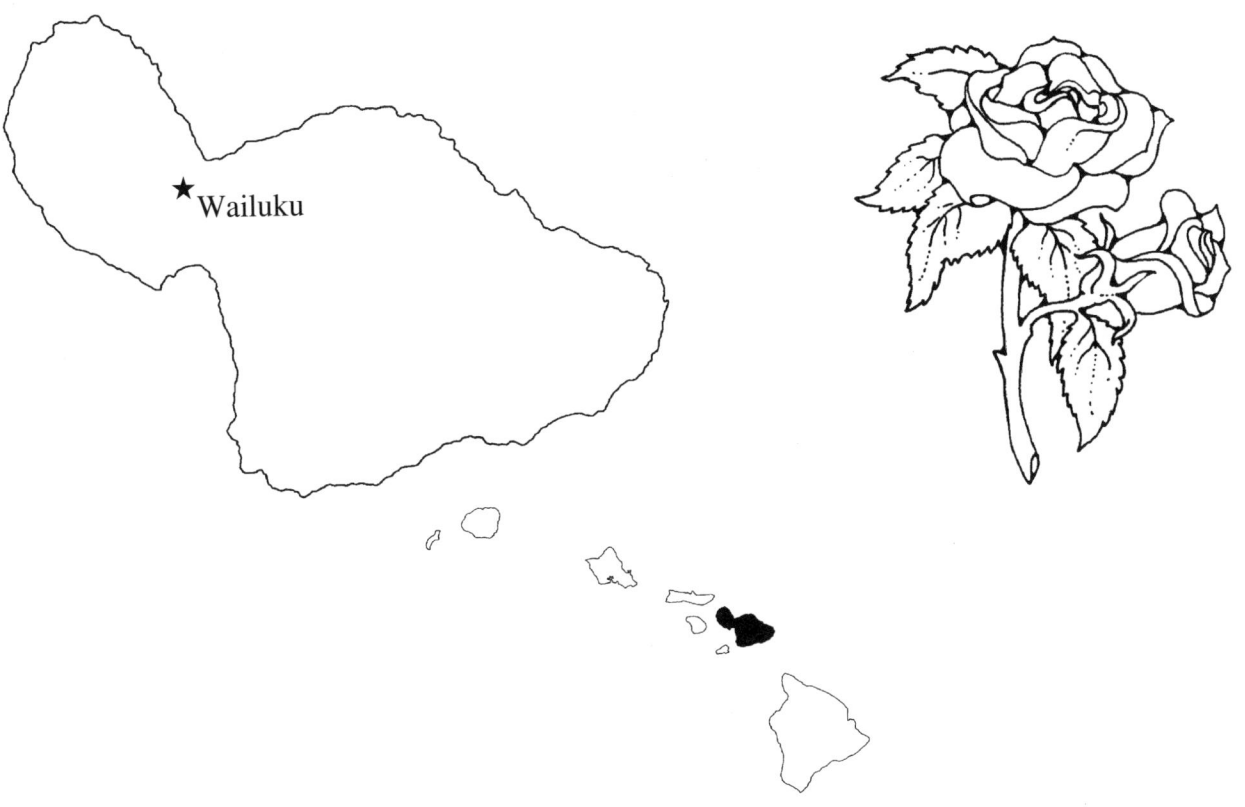

Maui Nō Ka ʻOi

words and music: Samuel Kapu

There is none like you,
Charming beyond compare,
Delighted are we with Haleakalā,
Maui, you are indeed the best.

Oʻahu

Waihoʻoluʻu: Melemele *Pua:* ʻIlima *Mele:* O Beautiful ʻIlima

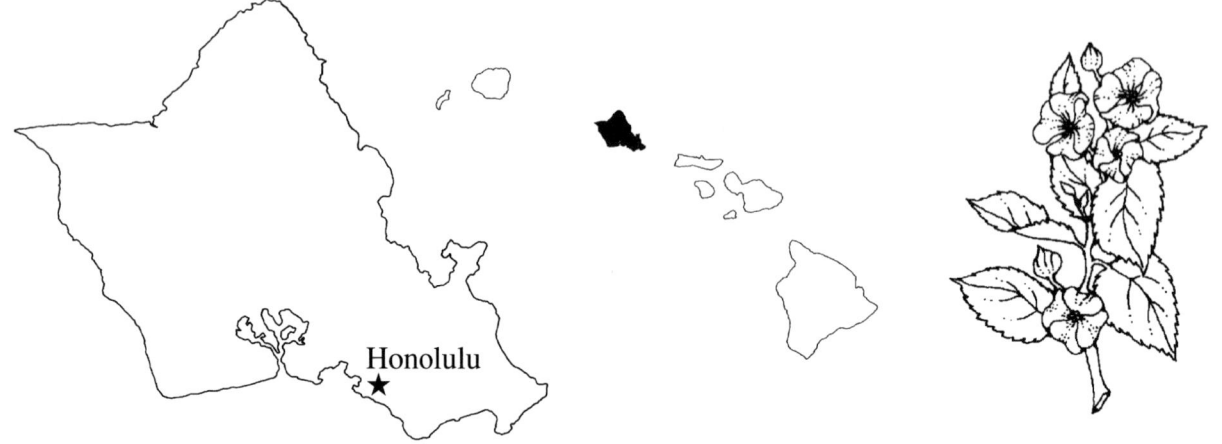

Aloha Oʻahu

words and music: Clarence Kinney

F
Aloha Oʻahu
Bb
Lei ka ʻilima
        G7
Kohu manu ʻōʻō
C7   F
Hulu melemele.

O Beautiful ʻIlima

words: Emma A.K. DeFries music: Henry Berger

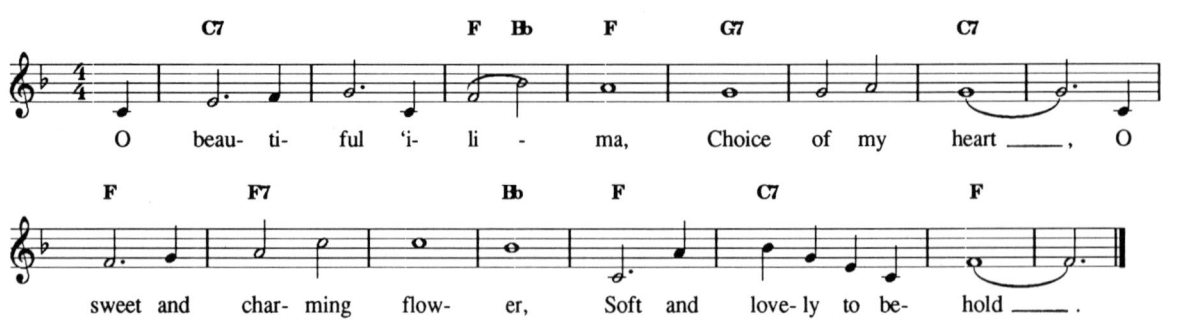

O beau-ti-ful ʻi-li-ma, Choice of my heart____, O sweet and char-ming flow-er, Soft and love-ly to be-hold____.

36

Kaua'i

Waiho'olu'u: Poni *Hua Li'ili'i:* Mokihana (a berry, not a flower) *Mele:* Maika'i Kaua'i

Maika'i Kaua'i

words and music: Henry Waia'u

Mai-ka-'i nō Kau-a-'i, He-mo-le-le i ka mā-li-e,
Ku-a-hi-wi Wai-'a-le-'a-le, Lei a-na i ka mo-ki-ha-na.
Mai-ka-'i wa-le nō Kau-a-'i, He-mo-le-le wa-le i ka mā-li-e,
Ku-a-hi-wi na-ni Wai-'a-le-'a-le, Lei a-na i ka mo-ki-ha-na.

Beautiful indeed is Kaua'i,
Blest with serenity,
Mount Wai'ale'ale,
Adorned with *mokihana*.

Very lovely indeed is Kaua'i,
So blest with serenity,
Beautiful mountain, Wai'ale'ale,
Adorned with *mokihana*.

Moloka'i

Waiho'olu'u: 'Ōma'oma'o | *Pua: Kukui* | *Mele:* Moloka'i Nui A Hina

Kaunakakai

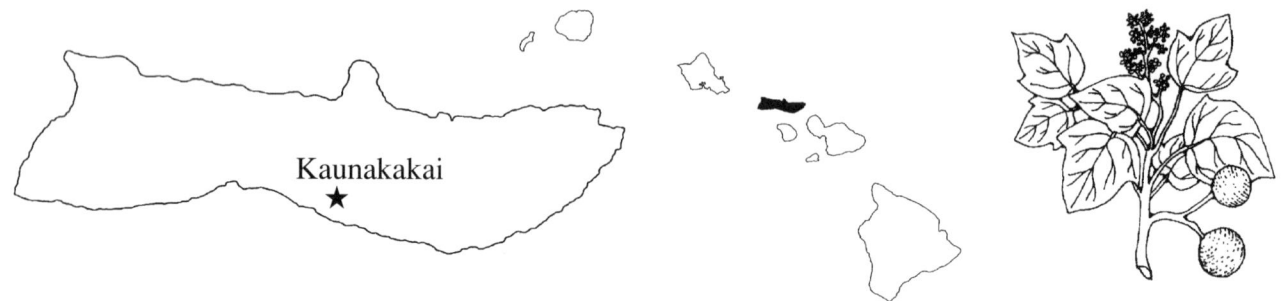

Moloka'i Nui A Hina

words and music: unknown

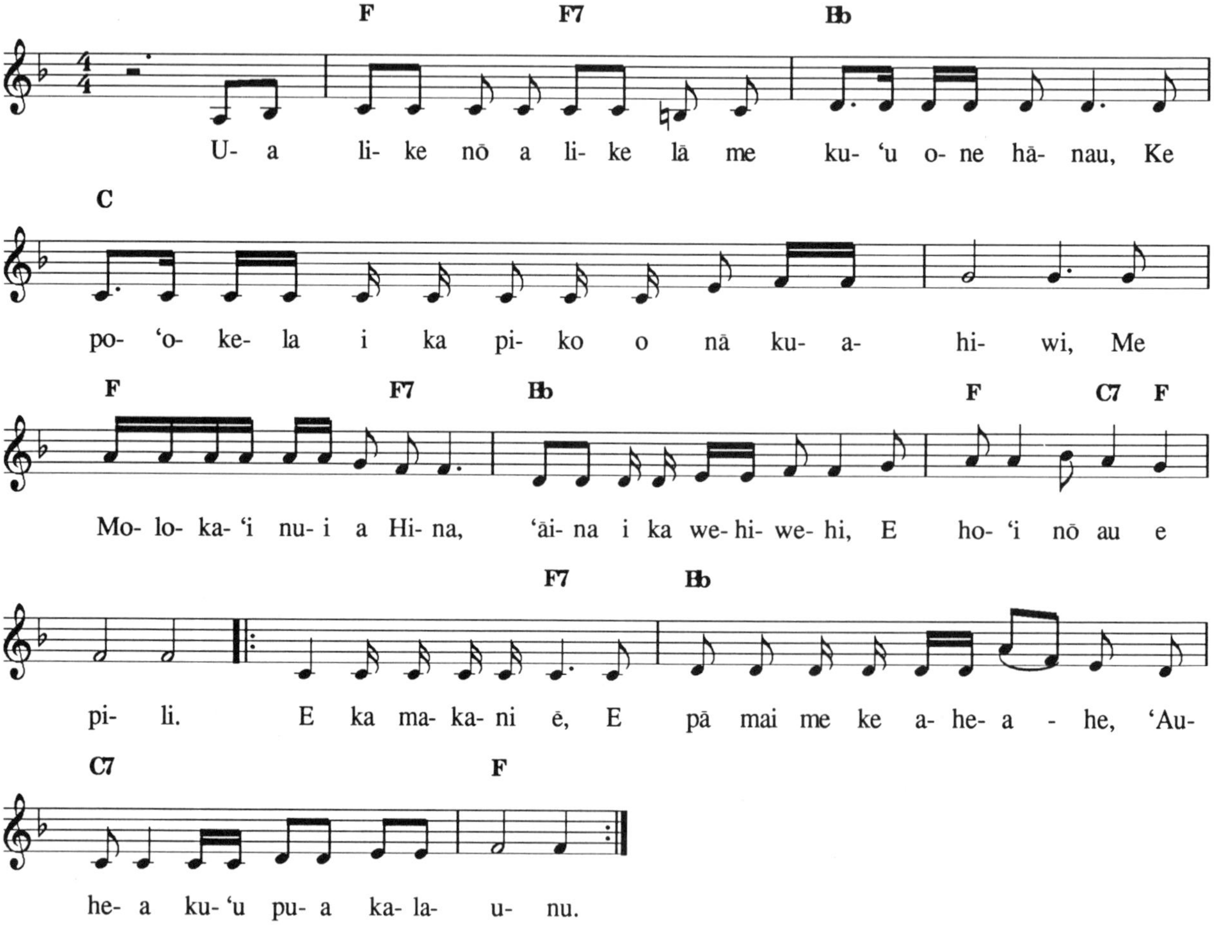

F F7 Bb
U- a li- ke nō a li- ke lā me ku- 'u o- ne hā- nau, Ke
C
po- 'o- ke- la i ka pi- ko o nā ku- a- hi- wi, Me
F F7 Bb F C7 F
Mo- lo- ka- 'i nu- i a Hi- na, 'āi- na i ka we- hi- we- hi, E ho- 'i nō au e
F7 Bb
pi- li. E ka ma- ka- ni ē, E pā mai me ke a- he- a - he, 'Au-
C7 F
he- a ku- 'u pu- a ka- la- u- nu.

That is exactly the way,
With the land of my birth,
The very top of the summit of the mountain,
Moloka'i, child of Hina,

Land adorned,
I shall return to be with you.
O wind, blowing gently hither,
Where is my crown flower?

Lāna'i

Waiho'olu'u: 'Alani *Pua:* Kauna'oa *Mele:* Lāna'i

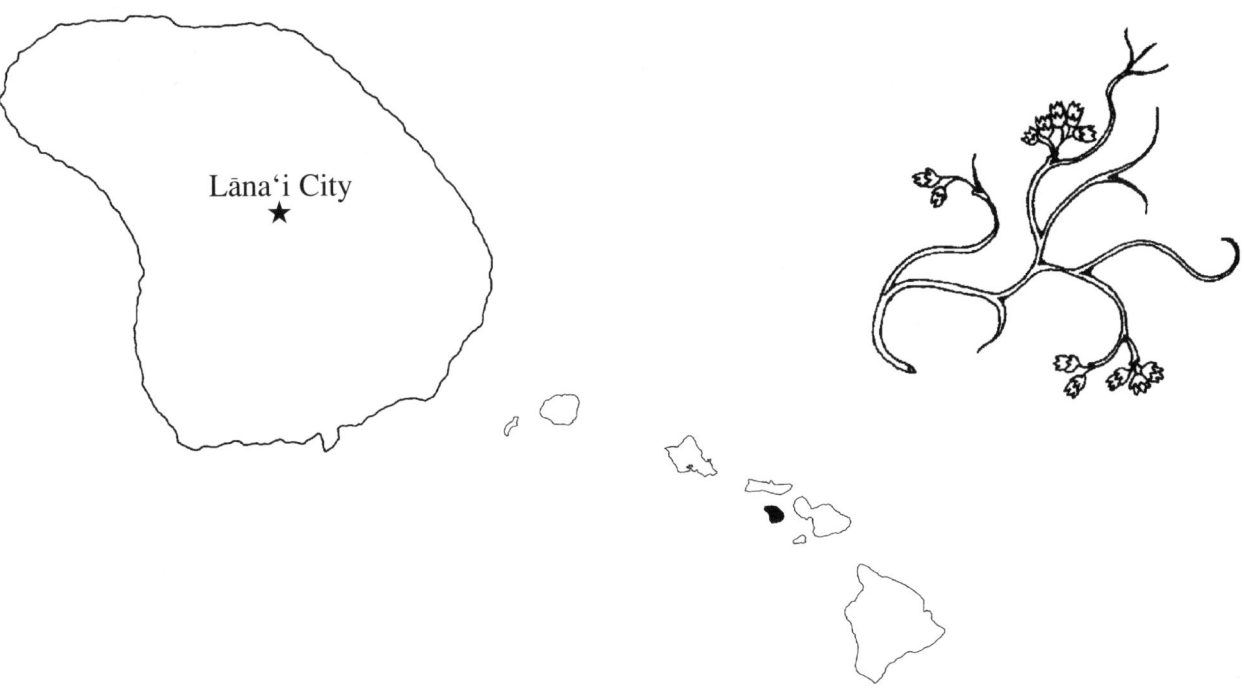

Lāna'i

words: Samuel Kapu
music: unknown

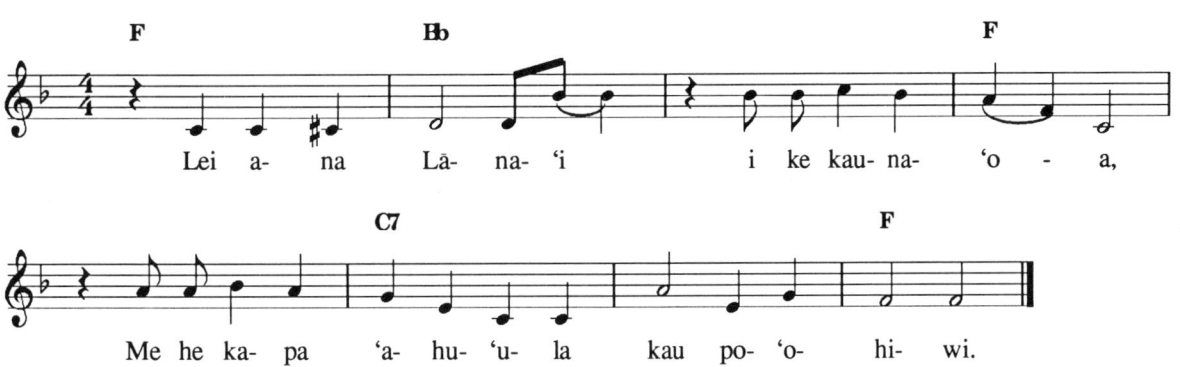

Lāna'i is bedecked with the *kauna'oa*
And a feather cloak placed on the shoulders.

Ni'ihau

Waiho'olu'u: Ke'oke'o   *Pua:* Pūpū (shells)   *Mele:* Pūpū o Ni'ihau

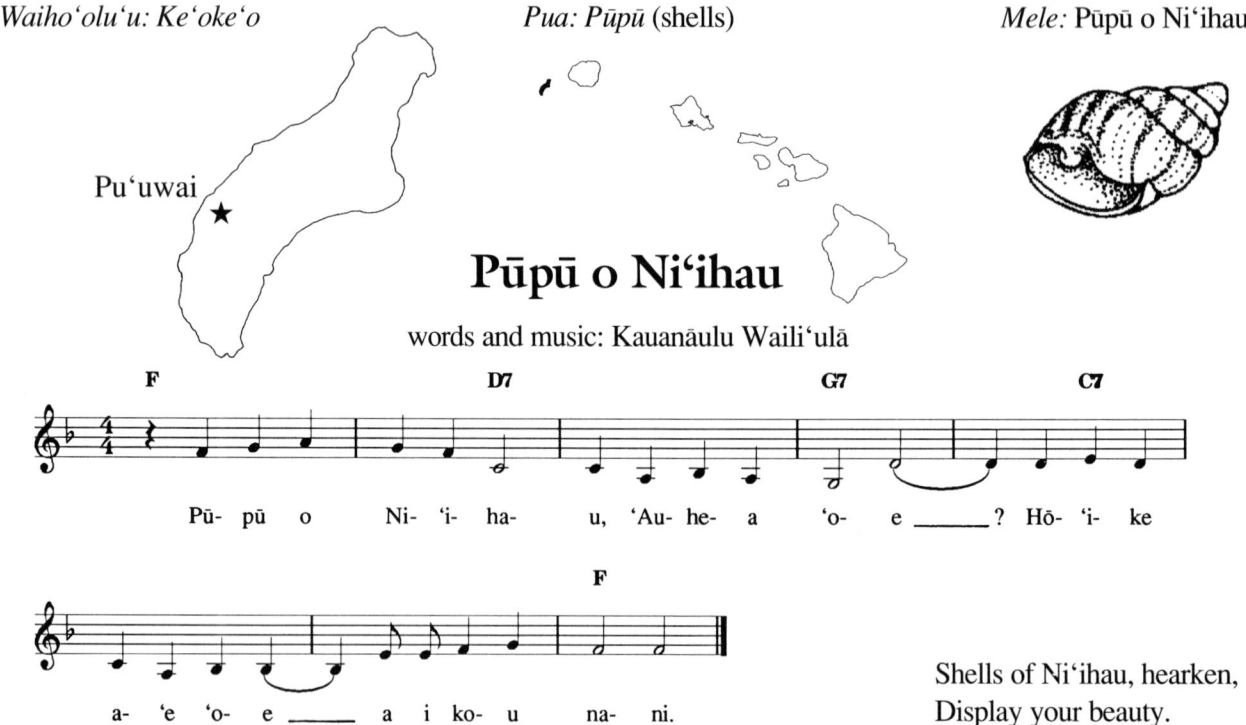

Pūpū o Ni'ihau

words and music: Kauanāulu Waili'ulā

Pū- pū o Ni- 'i- ha- u, 'Au- he- a 'o- e _____ ? Hō- 'i- ke a- 'e 'o- e _____ a i ko- u na- ni.

Shells of Ni'ihau, hearken,
Display your beauty.

Kaho'olawe

Waiho'olu'u: Hinahina   *Pua:* Hinahina   *Mele:* Sweet Lei Hinahina

Sweet Lei Hinahina

words and music: unknown

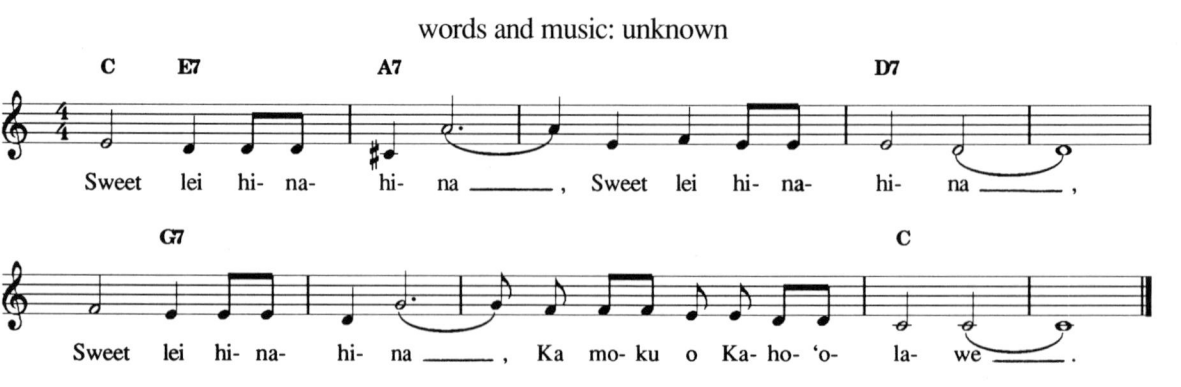

Sweet lei hi- na- hi- na _____ , Sweet lei hi- na- hi- na _____ ,
Sweet lei hi- na- hi- na _____ , Ka mo- ku o Ka- ho- 'o- la- we _____ .

Sweet *lei hinahina*, Sweet *lei hinahina*   Sweet *lei hinahina*, The island of Kaho'olawe.

Nā Mele Hoʻomākaʻikaʻi

songs of Explorations

E Hoʻomaikaʻi

words and music: unknown

```
C       C7   F        C        G7
E hoʻomaikaʻi e nā kamaiki, no kēia ʻai, no kēia ʻai,
C       C7   F        C        G7       C
E hoʻomaikaʻi e nā kamaiki, no kēia ʻai, no kēia ʻai.
    F   C
||:ʻĀmene:||
```

E Ke Akua

words and music: Mahela Rosehill

```
  C
||:E ke Akua,:||              Dearest Lord,
  G7    C
||:Mahalo nō,:||              Our thanks to thee,
||:Mahalo iā ʻoe:||           We especially thank thee,
  G7    C
||:No kēia ʻai:||             for this food
||:ʻĀmene:||                  Amen
```

Aloha Kakahiaka

words and music: unknown

```
F                         C7     F
Aloha kakahiaka, means good morning to you:
          F    F    F
(chorus) Aloha, aloha, aloha
Aloha ʻauinalā, means good afternoon to you: (chorus)
Aloha ahiahi, means good evening to you: (chorus)
```

He Inoa No Pauahi

words and music: Leleiōhoku

       F   F7
1. *Honi ana i ke anu, i ka mea huʻihuʻi,*
         Bb   F   C7
   Huʻi hewa i ka ʻili, i ka ua Pōʻaihala,
      F   F7
   Lei ana i ka mokihana, i ka wewehi o Kaiona,
    Bb   F   C7   F
   Līhau pue i ke anu, hauʻoki o Kaleponi.

2. *Hiaʻai ka welina, ka neneʻe a ka ʻōhelopapa,*
   Pupua i ka noe, mōhāhā i ke anu,
   Noho nō me ka ʻanoʻi, ka manaʻo iā loko,
   ʻO loko hana nui, pau ʻole i ke ana ʻia.

3. *A ka wailele o Niakala, ʻike i ka wai ānuenue,*
   I ka pōʻaiʻai a ka ʻohu, hāliʻi paʻa i laila,
   Pue ana i ka ʻehu wai, pupuʻu i ke koʻekoʻe,
   Eia iho ka mehana o ka poli o Hiʻilei.

4. *E ō e ka wahine hele lā o Kaiona,*
   Alualu wailiʻulā o ke kaha pua ʻōhai,
   ʻO ka ua lani pōlua, pō anu o ke Koʻolau,
   Kuʻu hoa o ka malu kī, malu kukui o Kahoʻiwai.

1. Braving the cold and all things with chill,
   Biting as they strive, braving also the rain,
   The glory of our land, adorned with *mokihana*,
   Is radiant in the snow of icy California.

2. Yearning for her, clinging closely as the mountain vine,
   Spreads and unfolds despite the mist and cold,
   There she stayed in greatest love, possessed of hidden thoughts,
   Exalted, high, never to be measured.

3. At the falls of Niagara where she saw the rainbow's arch,
   In the all-surrounding mist, shrouded tight about it,
   Chilled she was by the water vapor, and shriveled up with dampness,
   There she found the warmth aglowing in the bosom of Hiʻilei.

4. Respond, O lady in the sunshine of Kaiona,
   Who seeks the mirages amid the *ōhai* of the plain,
   In the pouring, the cold rain of Koʻolau,
   My companion in the sheltering ti and *kukui* of Kahoʻiwai.

Mele Pī'āpā

words and music: Kaipo Hale and Keoni Du Pont

                    D   A7   D

1. There are thirteen letters in the *pī'āpā*, the *pī'āpā*, the *pī'āpā*,

   There are thirteen letters in the *pī'āpā*,
     A7   D
   That's the Hawaiian alphabet.

2. The first five letters are known as vowels, known as vowels, known as vowels,
   The first five letters are known as vowels:
   A, E, I, O, U.

3. The last eight letters are consonants, the consonants, the consonants,
   Hē, Kē, Lā, Mū, Nū, Pī, Wē,
   And *'okina*, the glottal stop.

4. The *'okina* makes a stop in the vocal sound, the vocal sound, the vocal sound,
   The *'okina* makes a stop in the vocal sound,
   Like *'a'a, 'e'e, 'i'i, 'o'o, 'u'u.*

5. In addition to the thirteen letters, the thirteen letters, the thirteen letters,
   In addition to the thirteen letters,
   (Is) the *kahakō*, known as the macron.

6. The *kahakō* stresses a vowel sound, a vowel sound, a vowel sound,
   The *kahakō* stresses a vowel sound,
   Ā, Ē, Ī, Ō, Ū.

7. The "w-glide" occurs sometimes, occurs sometimes, occurs sometimes,
   The "w-glide" occurs sometimes,
   With the vowels *"O"* and *"U."*

8. When *"O"* is followed by another vowel, another vowel, another vowel,
   When *"O"* is followed by another vowel,
   The "w-glide" occurs.

9. *Koali* has the "w-glide," the "w-glide," the "w-glide,"
   Koali has the "w-glide,"
   K, O, A, L, I.

10. When *"U"* is followed by another vowel, another vowel, another vowel,
    When *"U"* is followed by another vowel,
    The "w-glide" occurs.

11. *'Uala* has the "w-glide," the "w-glide," the "w-glide,"
    'Uala has the "w-glide,"
    'Okina ('), U, A, L, A.

12. The *"W"* with the other three vowels, the other three vowels, the other three vowels,
    The *"W"* with the other three vowels,
    Can have a *"W"* or *"V"* sound.

13. *H, A, W, A, I, 'Okina ('), I, I, 'Okina ('), I, I, 'Okina ('), I,*
    H, A, W, A, I, 'Okina ('), I,
    Hawai'i or Hawai'i.

14. *Eia ka puana no ka pī'āpā, ka pī'āpā, ka pī'āpā,*
    Eia ka puana no ka pī'āpā,
    That's the Hawaiian alphabet.

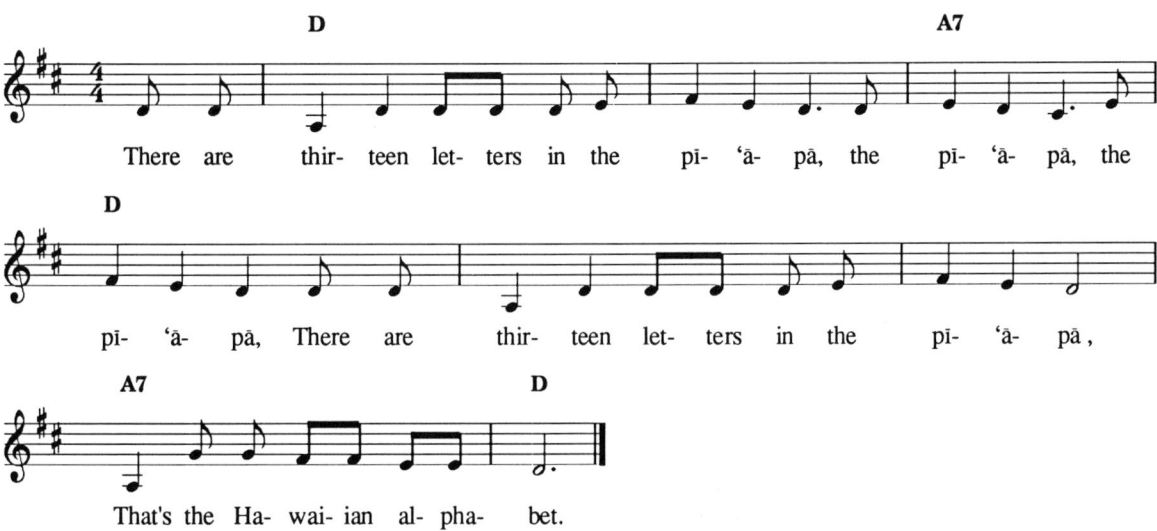

Eia Mākou

words and music: Kamuela Ka'ahanui

F	
Eia mākou, nā pua o Hawai'i!	Here we are, the children of Hawai'i!
C7	
Eia mākou, nā keiki ho'okani!	Here we are, the merry music makers!
F F7 Bb	
Eia mākou, nā alaka'i nani!	Here we are, the leaders of tomorrow!
F C7 F	
'Oli ē 'oli ē, no mākou!	Come along and join in our song!

E Ola Mau Ka ʻŌlelo Hawaiʻi*

words and music: Lopeka Kahakalau

E hele kākou i ka papa Hawaiʻi i Kamehameha
He papa Hawaiʻi no ke kūkā ʻana o ka ʻōlelo Hawaiʻi

ʻO ka ʻōlelo nō hoʻi ka mea nui na ka poʻe āpau
E ola mau ka ʻōlelo Hawaiʻi e ola mau a mau
E ola mau ka ʻōlelo Hawaiʻi e ola mau a mau

ʻO ka ʻōlelo nō hoʻi ka mea nui na ka poʻe āpau
E ola mau ka ʻōlelo Hawaiʻi e ola mau a mau
E ola mau ka ʻōlelo Hawaiʻi e ola mau a mau

*adapted for *Explorations/Hoʻomākaʻikaʻi: 1991* by Warren Kekauoha, Kāhealani Naeʻole and Keoma Akau

Hana Wau I ka Ipu

words and music: Holoua Stender

Hana wau i ka ipu heke ʻole,
I ka ipu heke ʻole,
Hana wau i ka ipu heke ʻole,
I ka papa hana noʻeau.

Hana wau i ka ʻohe hano ihu,
I ka ʻohe hano ihu,
Hana wau i ka ʻohe hano ihu,
I ka papa hana noʻeau.

Hana wau i ka mea kanu ipu,
I ka mea kanu ipu,
Hana wau i ka mea kanu ipu,
I ka papa hana noʻeau.
Pau ka hana, hoʻi ana, ua lawa, ua pau!

Ko Kula Uka, Ko Kula Kai

words and music: L. Keʻala Kwan

Ko kula uka, ko kula kai
Mahalo (e) ke Akua no nā mea waiwai
Ko kula uka, ko kula kai
Mahalo aku, mahalo mai.

Ko kula uka, ko kula kai
Aia nā mea, nā mea waiwai
Ko kula uka, ko kula kai
Māhele aku, māhele mai.

Ko kula uka, ko kula kai
E mau ana nō nā mea waiwai
Ko kula uka, ko kula kai
Aloha aku, aloha mai.

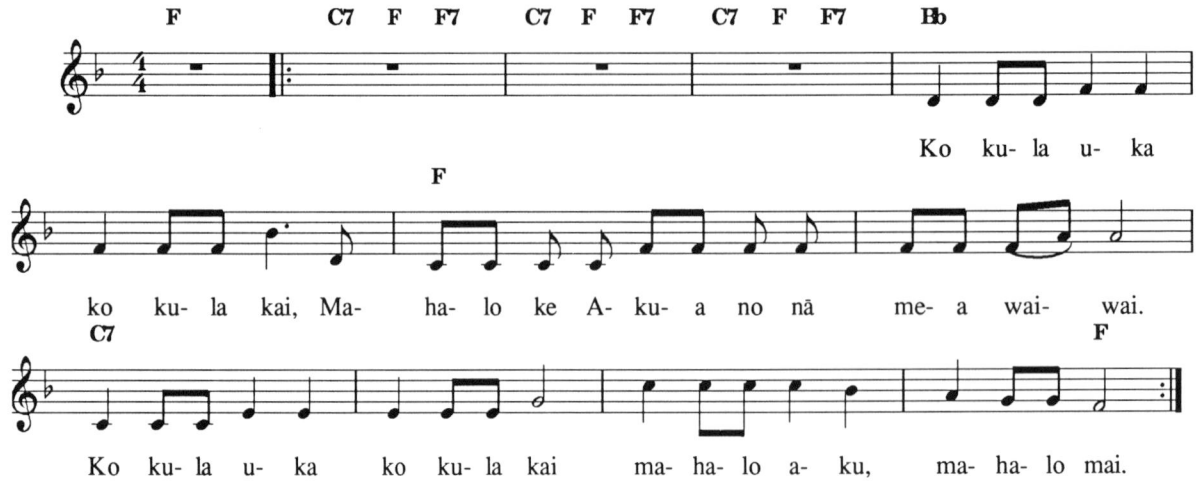

Nani Ka'ala

words and music: traditional

He nani Ka'ala, lae la lae lae	Pretty Ka'ala, tra la la
Kuahiwi nani 'oe, lae la lae lae	You are a beautiful mountain, tra la la
I Nu'uanu au, lae la lae lae	I was at Nu'uanu, tra la la
Ka makani Ko'olau, lae la lae lae	In the tradewinds, tra la la
I Honolulu au, lae la lae lae	I was at Honolulu, tra la la
Hale Ali'i o 'Iolani, lae la lae lae*	'Iolani home of the *Ali'i*, tra la la
I Ala Moana au, lae la lae lae	I was at Ala Moana, tra la la
Hoe ana i ka wa'a, lae la lae lae*	Paddling the canoe, tra la la
I Makapu'u au, lae la lae lae	I was at Makapu'u, tra la la
Nā i'a i ke kai, lae la lae lae*	Fishes swimming in the sea, tra la la
I Lā'ie au, lae la lae lae	I was at Lā'ie, tra la la
Me nā po'e Pākīpika, lae la lae lae*	With the Pacific people, tra la la
Ha'ina ka puana, lae la lae lae	Tell the refrain
Kuahiwi nani 'oe, lae la lae lae	You are the beautiful mountain, tra la la

*New verses composed for *Explorations/Ho'omāka'ika'i: 1992*
Ala Moana, Honolulu and Makapu'u: Holoua Stender; Lā'ie: L. Ke'ala Kwan

Makalapua

words: Queen Liliʻuokalani
music: Eliza Holt

The Queen's Prayer

words and music: Queen Liliʻuokalani

G	
ʻO kou aloha nō	O! Lord Thy loving mercy,
C D7	
Aia i ka lani,	Is high as the heavens,
G C	
Aʻo kou ʻoiaʻiʻo	It tells us of Thy truth
D7 G	
He hemolele hoʻi.	And ʼtis filled with holiness.

The 'Ukulele
Our Adopted String Instrument

'uku (flea) *lele* (jumping)

How to tune your *'ukulele*

1. By piano . . . . . G, C, E, A
2. By ear . . . . . So, Do, Mi, La

How to play your *'ukulele*

strumming—common stroke:
a. Relax wrist to allow free down and up movement.
b. Arm remains quiet
c. Using first finger, strum down gently, following upward on fleshy cushion of finger

Parts of the *'ukulele*

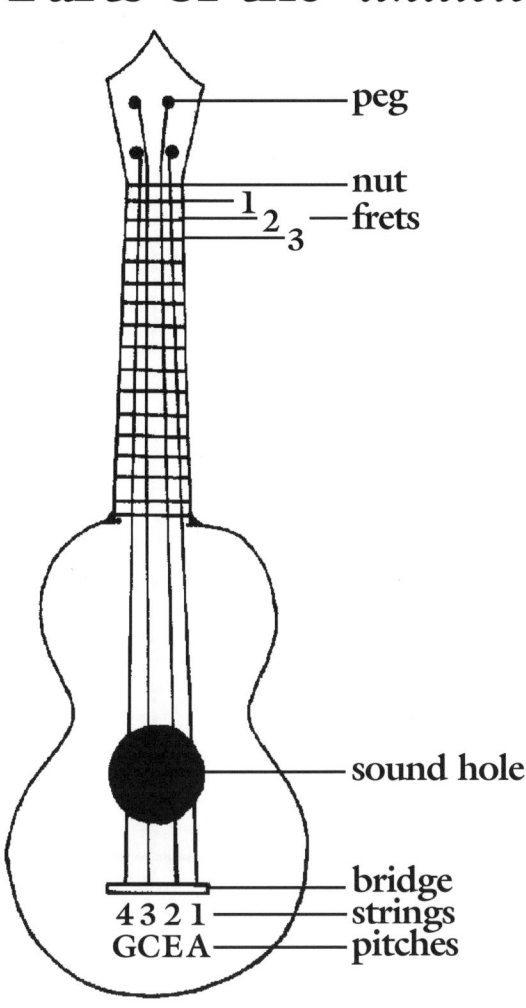

fingering

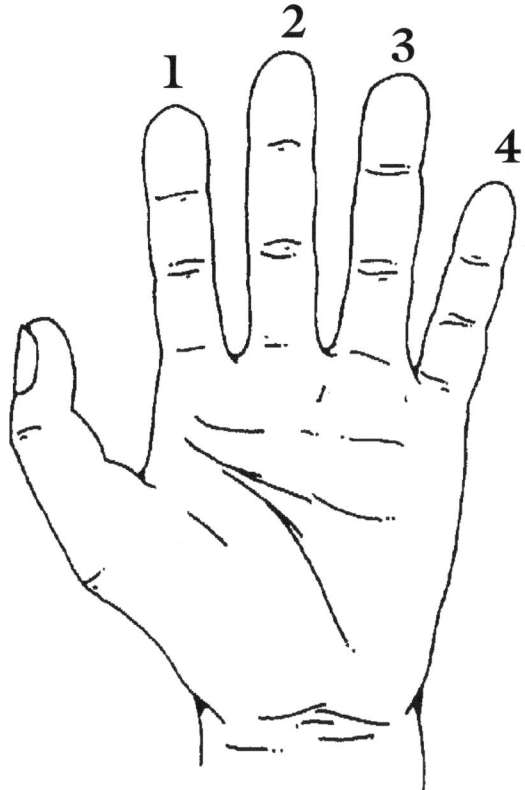

CAPITAL LETTERS = Major chord
small letters = Minor chord

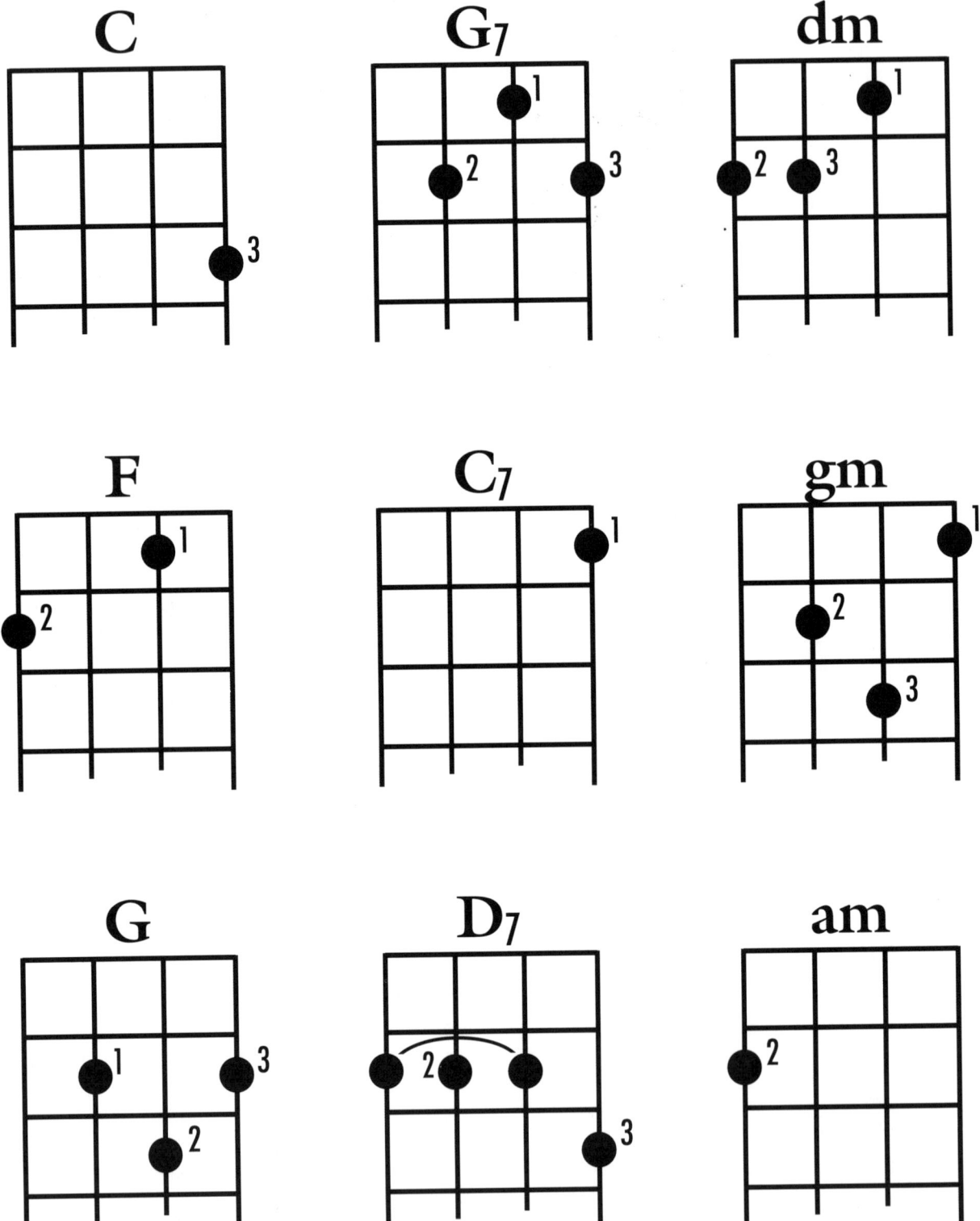

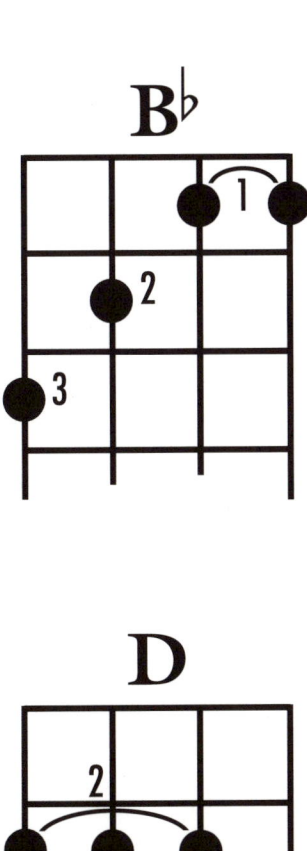
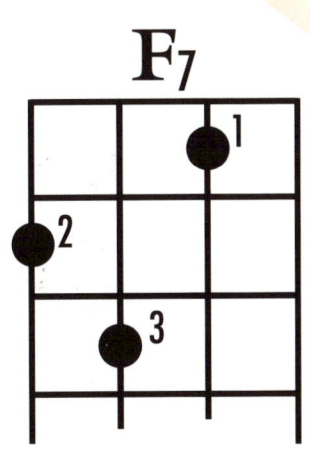
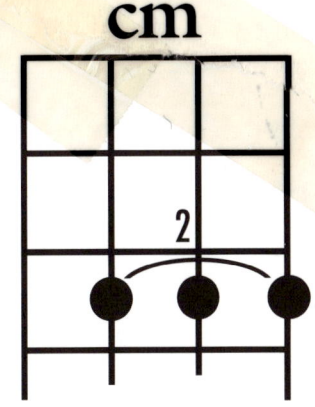
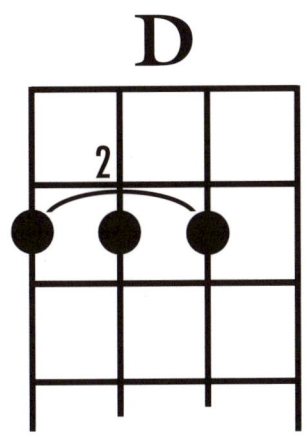
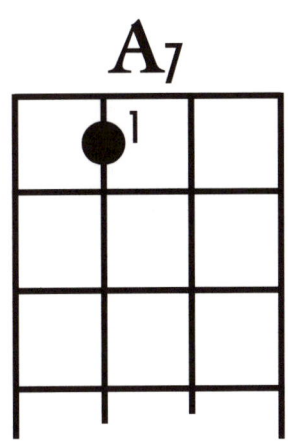
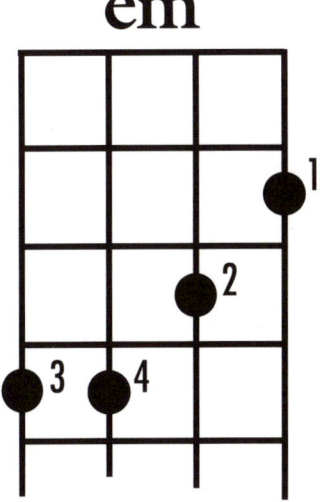
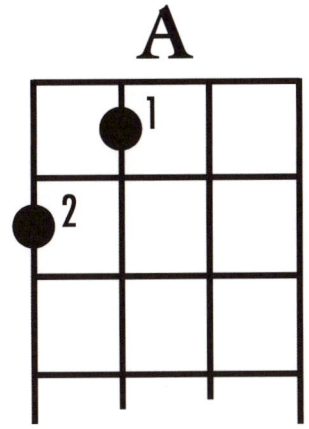
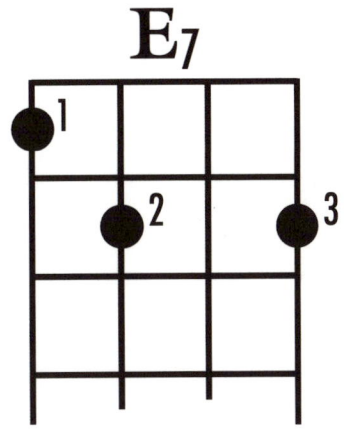
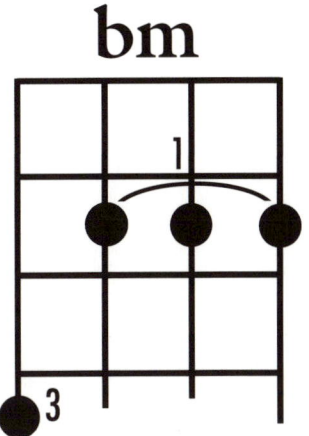

Ka ʻŌlelo Hawaiʻi

The Hawaiian Language

In our study of the Hawaiian language in Hoʻomākaʻikaʻi this year we will be using various kinds of materials. Our three language lessons deal with:

ka hoʻolauna ʻana (greetings and basic Hawaiian words)
nā māhele o ke kino (parts of the body)
ka ʻohana (the extended family)

We also have a *moʻolelo* (story) and will be learning *ʻōlelo noʻeau* (wise sayings) of our *kūpuna* (elders) and *mele* (songs) to accompany our lessons.

With all of these things planned, by the end of our week we will all be able to sing, dance, play and speak in the real Hawaiian way.

E hoʻomaka kākou! (Let us begin!)

Ka Hoʻolauna ʻAna
greetings and basic Hawaiian words

ʻae	yes
ʻaʻole	no
ʻāwīwī	hurry
e hana hou; e ʻōlelo hou	repeat action; repeat saying
e hoʻolohe ka pepeiao	listen
e nānā ka maka	look at
e paʻa ka waha	quiet
e paʻa ka waha a e hana me ka lima	be quiet and do your work
haumāna	student
he mea iki	it's a little thing (you're welcome)
hoʻomākaukau	get ready
kali	wait
kāne	man
kumu	teacher
mākaukau?	ready?
nā kamaliʻi	children
wahine	woman

maikaʻi
(good)

auē!
(my goodness!)

a hui hou
(good-bye)

aloha kakahiaka
(good morning)

aloha awakea
(good noonday)

aloha ʻauinalā
(good afternoon)

aloha ahiahi
(good evening)

Nā Māhele o ke Kino
parts of the body

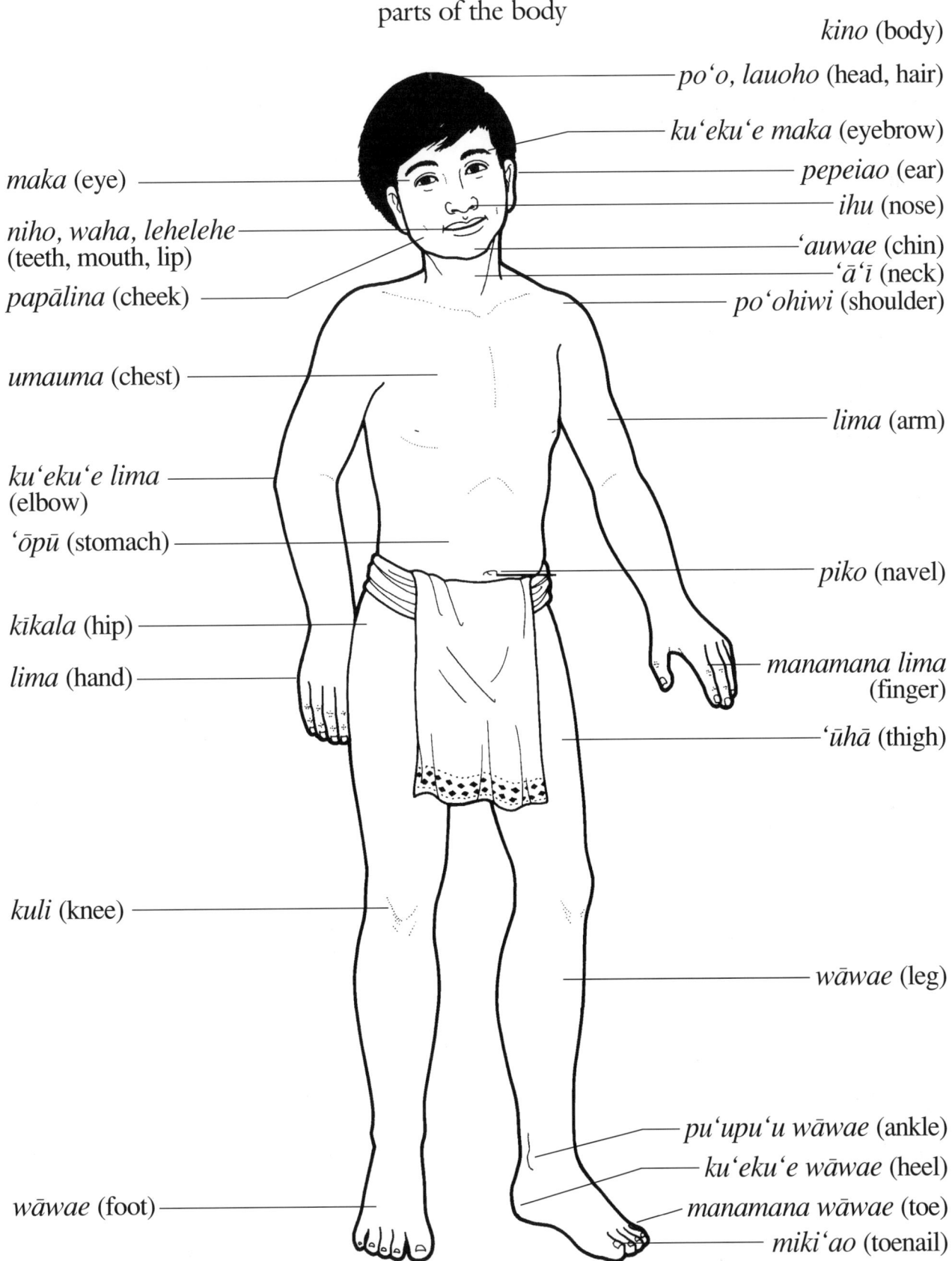

59

Ka ʻOhana
the extended family

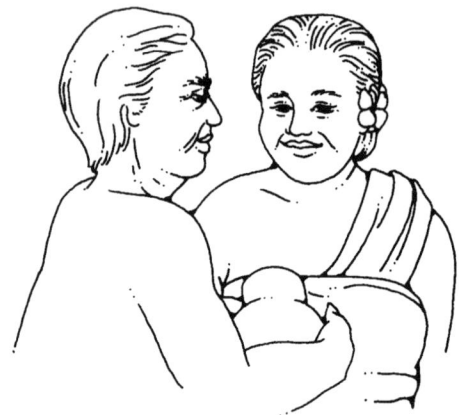

kūpuna
(grandparents)

kupuna kāne
(grandfather)

mākua
(parents)

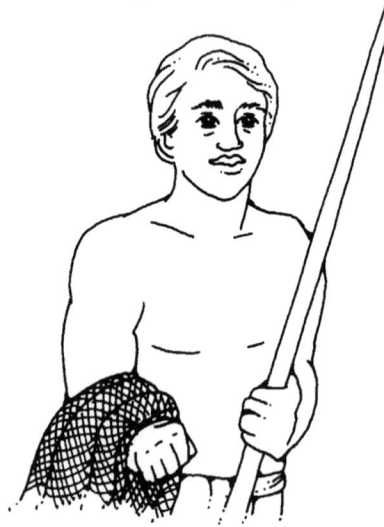

makua kāne
(father)

kamaliʻi
(children)

keiki kāne
(son, boy)

kupuna wahine
(grandmother)

makuahine
(mother)

kaikamahine
(daughter, girl)

'ohana
(extended family)

keiki
(child, baby)

"The Young Chief's Companions"

Word List

kamaliʻi ....children
kanaka ....man
keiki ....child
keiki kāne ....son
lima ....hand
makua kāne ....father
makuahine ....mother
nā keiki kāne ....boys, sons
nā mākua ....parents
pēpē ....baby
poʻo ....head
wahine ....wife

The Young Chief's Companions

The ruling chief of Maui gave his first-born **son** to the keeping of a trusted warrior and his **wife**. Many days passed and the chief longed for his baby. "I shall go secretly," he told himself, "and see whether my son has the care that a young chief should have."

So the ruler came to the Moloka'i village where that warrior lived. He came alone, paddling a single canoe. He found the warrior's home and, nearby in a shady spot, he saw two little boys. One held a **baby**, the chief's **son**, while the other fed the little one. What was the food he was putting, bit by bit, into the **child's** mouth? Unnoticed the chief drew closer. *Kalo* (taro) tops, cooked *kalo* tops! Was that food fit for a young chief? The father was filled with rage.

"Where are your **parents**?" he demanded in loud tones.

The little **boys** glanced up, surprised at the sight of a tall stranger. "Our **father** is working in the *kalo* patch," said the older boy quietly. "Our mother has gone to the forest for bark to dye her *kapa* (tapa)."

"And is there no fish," the chief asked, "that you feed that child with *kalo* tops?"

"There is much fish," the **boy** replied. "But this little one is a young chief and very precious. 'If he cries, feed him,' our **father** said. 'Feed him cooked *kalo* tops, not fish, lest he choke on a bone and die.'"

63

The **boys** paid no more attention to the stranger, but continued to feed the **baby** till he was satisfied and fell asleep. Then the older **boy** laid him carefully on a mat. The chief watched every movement. He saw that both the **boys** treated the **child** with great respect. The older held the **baby** carefully, but never once placed his **hand** above the **head** of the little chief. With a grunt of satisfaction the ruler left the **children** and returned to his canoe.

When their **father** came, the **boys** told him they had taken good care of the precious **baby**. "A **man** was here," said one, "a tall stranger who came in a canoe. He watched us feed the little chief, then went away."

Our ruler! thought the **father**. Had he been satisfied or angry at what he saw?

Later the chief sent for this warrior. "Let my **son** return to his home," was his command, "and send your **boys** to serve him. Your **sons** shall be attendants and companions of the little chief, for I have watched them. Like you, they can be trusted."

From a Hawaiian newspaper,
translated by
Mary Kawena Pūkuʻi

Ka Mahiʻai
the planter

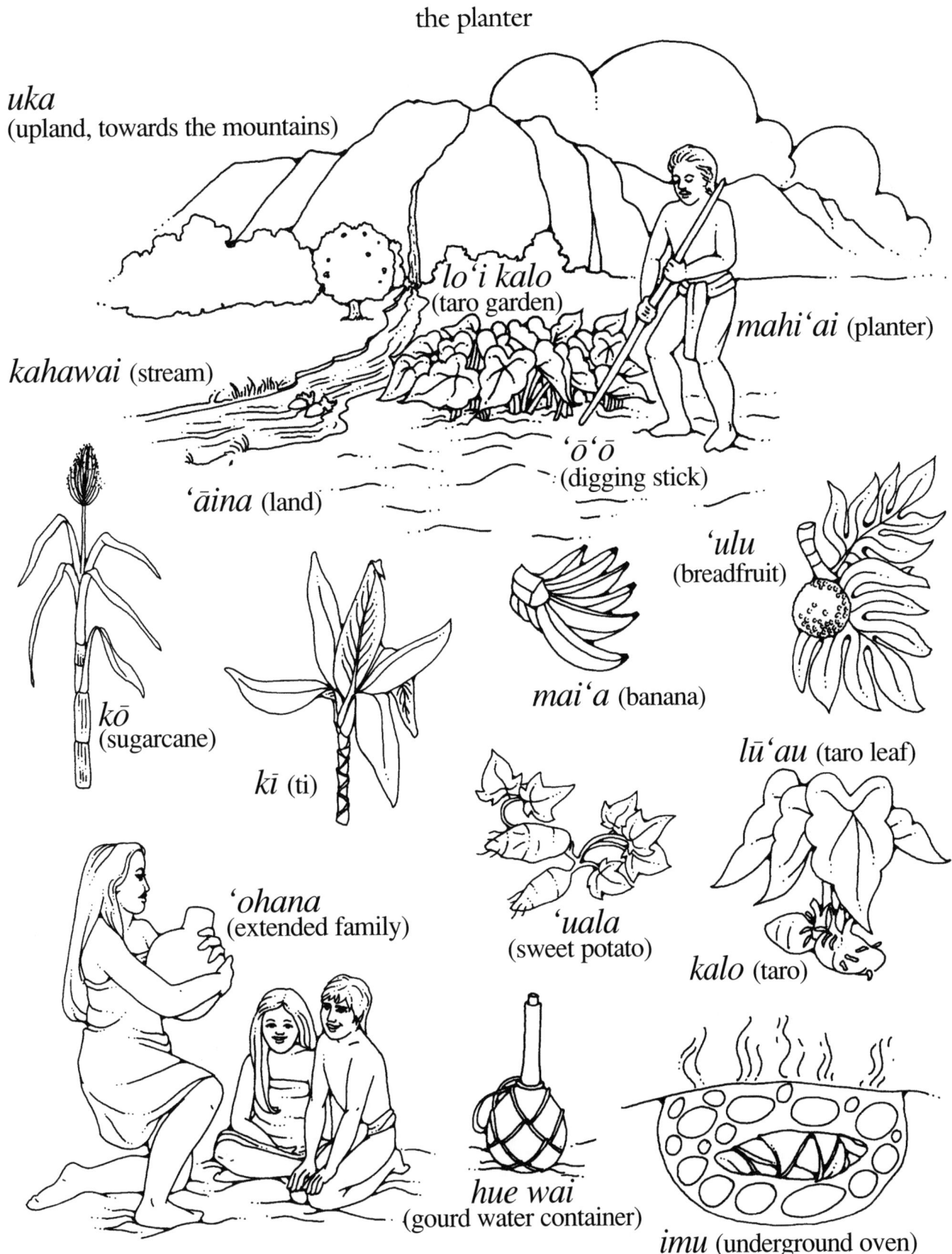

Ka Lawaiʻa
the fisherman

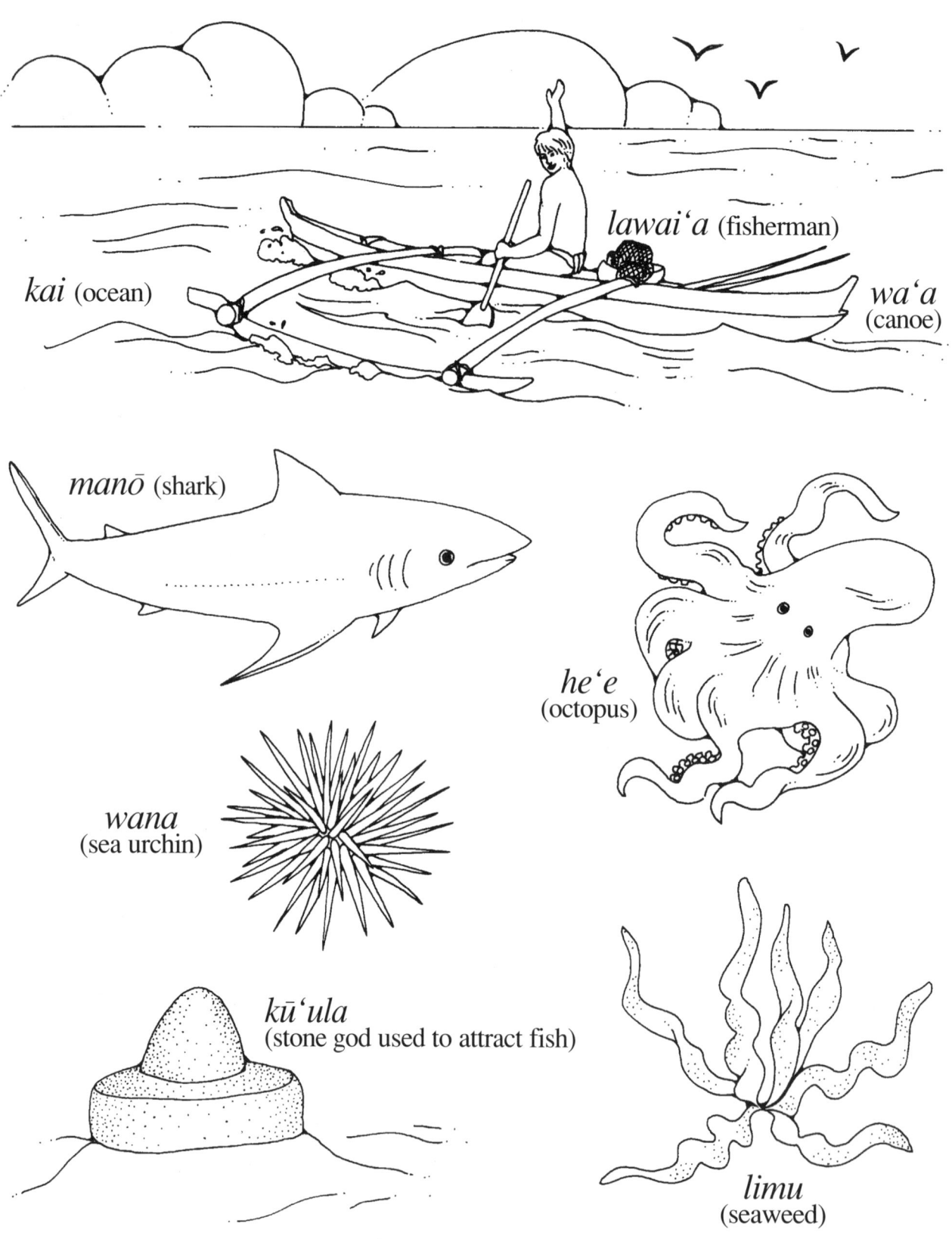

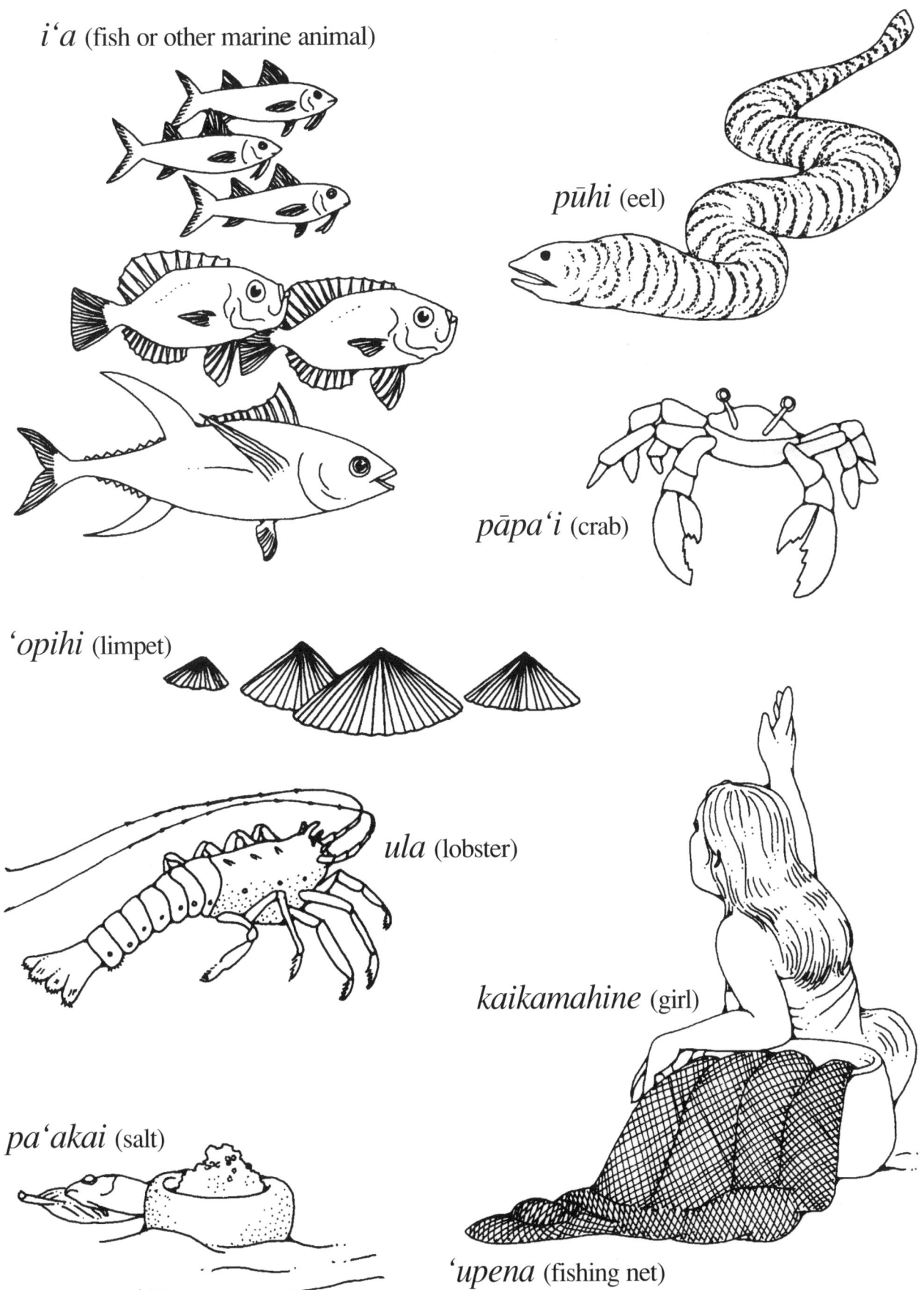

Nā ʻŌlelo Noʻeau
the wise sayings

Aia i ka ʻōlelo ke ola a me ka make.
In language is life and death.

E aloha kekahi i kekahi.
Love one another.

E kaupē aku nō i ka hoe a kō mai.
Put the paddle forward and draw it back.

E mālama i ka ʻāina, na ka ʻāina e hānai iā kākou.
Care for the land and the land will provide for us.

E mālama i ke kai.
Take care of the sea.

E mālama ʻia nā pono o ka ʻāina e nā ʻōpio.
The traditions of the land are perpetuated by its youth.

E makaʻala kākou.
We are alert.

Ka ikaika o ka manaʻo me ke kino.
Be strong in mind and body.

Kūlia e loaʻa ka naʻauao.
Strive to obtain wisdom.

Kūlia i ka lōkahi i ke ola.
Strive for harmony in life.

Mai makaʻu i ka hana. Makaʻu i ka moloā.
Do not fear work. Fear laziness.

Many more of these can be found in *ʻŌlelo Noʻeau: Hawaiian Proverbs and Poetical Sayings* by Mary Kawena Pūkuʻi, Bishop Museum Press (1983).

Nā Mele

Eia Koʻu Kino
words: Lurline Naone Salvador

Hoʻomākaukau
Kāhea—Eia Koʻu Kino
Pā

Eia ke poʻo
(me nā maka)

Eia ka waha
(me nā niho)

Eia nā lima
(manamana lima)

Eia ka ʻōpū
(me ka piko)

Eia nā wāwae
(me nā kuli)

Eia nā māhele o koʻu kino.

Here's My Body

Get ready
Call—Here's My Body
Begin

Here's the head
(with the eyes)

Here's the mouth
(with the teeth)

Here are the hands
(and fingers)

Here's the stomach
(with the navel)

Here are the legs
(with the knees)

Here are the parts of my body.

Kahi Olonā
words and music: unknown

Hoʻomākaukau
Kāhea—Kahi Olonā
Pā

Kahi, lua, kolu, hā, lima, ono, hiku, walu, iwa, ʻumi

1. *Kahi—kahi olonā*
2. *Lua—lua ʻōhiki*
3. *Kolu—kolu kaimana*
4. *Hā—hāhā ʻōpae*
5. *Lima—lima pūhō*
6. *Ono—ʻono meaʻono*
7. *Hiku—Nā hiku o Makaliʻi*
8. *Walu—alualu kao*
9. *Iwa—ʻiwa kiani*
10. *ʻUmi—ʻumiʻumi kao*

Kahi, lua, kolu, hā, lima, ono, hiku, walu, iwa, ʻumi!

To Scrape *Olonā*
(Counting Chant)

Get ready
Call—Scraping *Olonā*
Begin

to scrape *olonā*
crab hole
three diamonds
to feel for shrimp
sore on the hand
delicious dessert
group of stars
to chase a goat
ʻiwa bird soaring
goat's beard

Eia Ke Kaula
(Hei)

words: Nona Beamer

Hoʻomākaukau
Kāhea—Eia Ke Kaula
Pā

Eia ke kaula (kaula, kaula)
Lōʻihi ke kaula
(kaula, kaula)
Hana i ke kaula
(kaula, kaula)
Nā manamana lima
(lima, lima)
Mana lima nui (nui, nui)
Lima liʻiliʻi (liʻi, liʻi)
Nānā i ka hei (hei, hei)

Huli i ka hei (hei, hei)
ʻIke i nā maka nui (nui, nui)
ʻIke i ka ihu nui (nui, nui)
Eia mai . . .

A e pau aʻela nō!

Here is the String
(String figure for two eyes)

Get ready
Call—Here's The String
Begin

Here is the string,
Long is the string,

Work with the string,

With the fingers,

And the thumb,
And the baby finger,
Look at the *hei* (string figure)

Turn the *hei*,
See the big eyes,
See the big nose
Here is it . . .

And it is finished.

Nā Hula

Hawaiian Dances

Hula is Hawaiian dance that tells a story through chant and gestures. The story may be one that honors a god, a goddess or an *aliʻi* (chief or ruler). It may be about a place or a thing.

To become a dancer in old Hawaiʻi meant a long and strict course of training under a *kumu hula* (teacher of *hula*). The *haumāna* (students) were taught in the *hālau hula* (meeting house, or school, for *hula*). An altar was built inside the *hālau*. The *haumāna* placed gifts of *lei* (garlands or wreaths) at the altar. They chanted greetings and praises to Laka, goddess of the *hula*.

At the end of the training period an *ʻūniki* (graduation) was held. After the ceremony the dancers were ready to perform before the *aliʻi* and the people.

According to the oldest *mele* (song) the goddess Hōpoe was the first *kumu hula*. Hōpoe's first *haumāna* or student was Hi'iakaikapoliopele. This was Pele's youngest and favorite sister, Hi'iaka. Today chants for Pele are commemorated in the name of Hi'iaka.

Hula has become a form of entertainment for all people. Both men and women dance. They can perform either sitting or standing.

An *'ōlapa* (standing dancer) is usually accompanied by a *ho'opa'a* (seated chanter-drummer). The *ho'opa'a* beats the *ipu hula* (gourd drum) for some dances. For other dances the *pahu* (wooden drum with a sharkskin head) is used.

A seated dancer usually does his own chanting. At the same time he accompanies himself with a *hula* instrument.

Dancers begin and end each *hula* with a *kāhea* (call). The *kāhea* at the beginning is either the title or the first line of the mele. The *kāhea* at the end is the dedication to the place, thing or person for which or whom the *mele* is composed. Dancers will sometimes *kāhea* the first word of the following verse while performing.

There is a basic vocabulary of hand gestures. The dancer depicts the world around him as he sees it in relation to himself. For example the motions for the things of the sea place the hands below the waist. The motions for the sun, moon, stars and clouds are placed above the head. The gestures for rain would start high and gradually be lowered in much the same way that rain really falls.

Hula Instruments

pahu hula
(wooden drum with a sharkskin head)

Sit before the pahu and strike the drum head with both hands, using the fingers and heel of the hand.

ʻūlili
(three gourds pierced by a stick)

Pull the string to twirl the gourds.

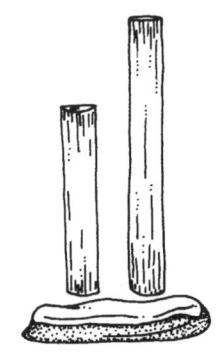

kāʻekeʻeke
(bamboo pipes)

Hold one bamboo pipe vertically in each hand, tapping down on the ground or on a stone padded by a mat or a folded piece of *kapa*.

papa hehi (footboard)

Tip and tap the board with the foot to keep time. Use with *kā lāʻau* (rhythm sticks).

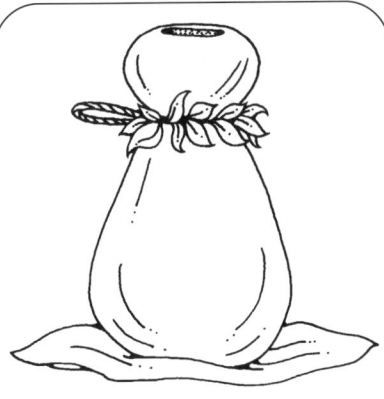

ipu hula
(gourd drum)

While seated, support the gourd with the wrist loop and left hand and thump the bottom down on the floor. Strike the side or bottom of the gourd with the fingers and palm of the right hand.

kā lāʻau
(rhythm sticks)

Hold the long rod in the left hand close to the body and strike it with the short rod.

pūniu
(coconut-shell drum)
and
kā (beater)

While seated tie the coconut-shell drum to the right thigh above the knee and strike the fish-skin head with a fiber thong.

Hula Pa‘i Umauma
chest-slapping dance

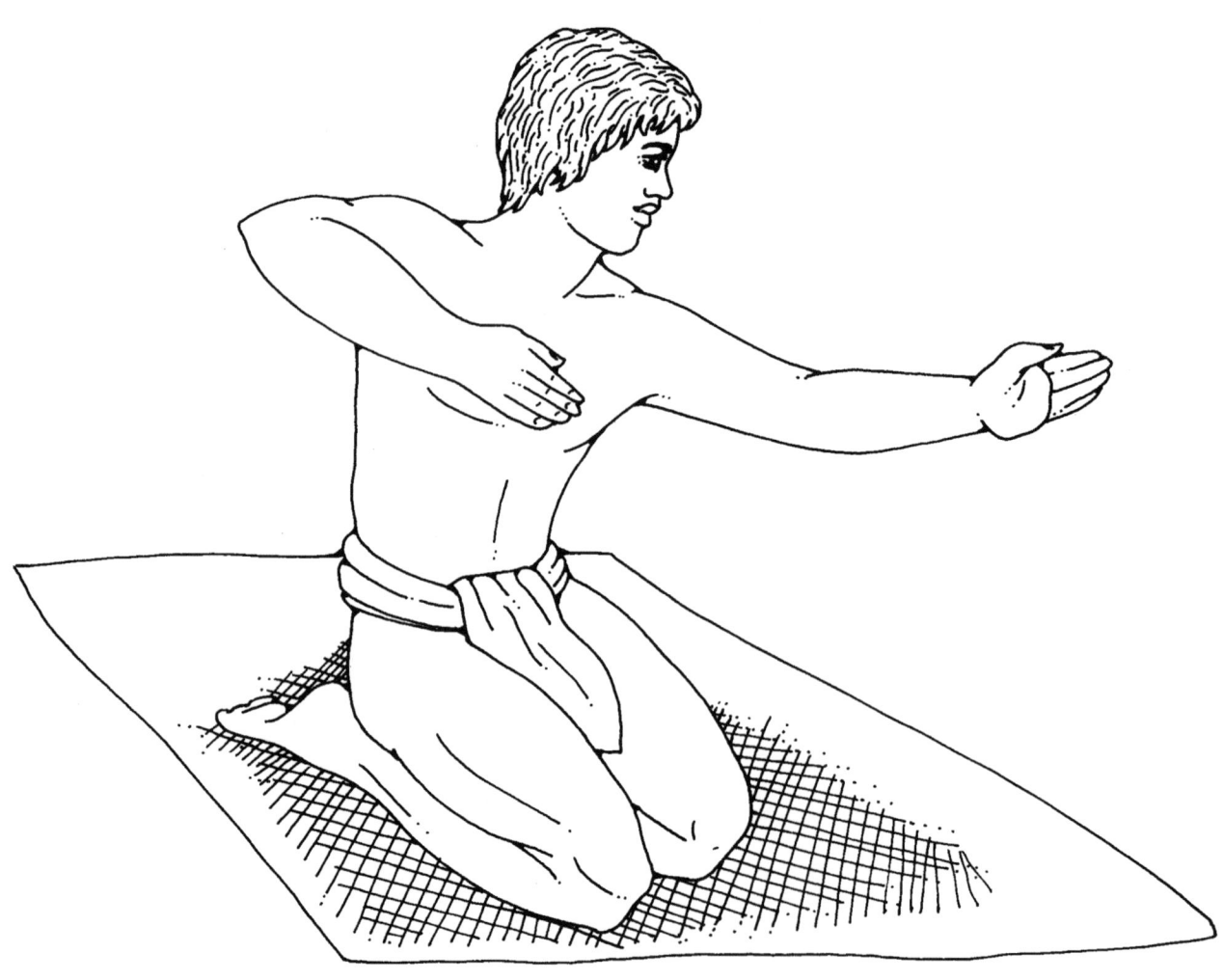

For the *hula pa‘i umauma* the dancer *pa‘i* (slaps) his *umauma* (chest) and the tops of both thighs with the palms of both hands in a definite rhythmic pattern.

Hula ʻIliʻili
pebble dance

For the *hula ʻiliʻili* two pairs of smooth water-worn lava pebbles are clicked together in a manner similar to Spanish castanets. One pebble is held tightly between the thumb and index finger and the other pebble lies flat along the three fingers. This last pebble is moved upward to click with the first pebble.

Hula Pā Ipu
gourd dance

For the *hula pā ipu* the dancer will hold the *ipu* with his left hand and *pa'i* it with his right hand in a definite rhythmic pattern.

Hula Kā Lāʻau
stick dance

For the *hula kā lāʻau* two hardwood sticks of the same length are struck together rhythmically throughout the chant. The dancer holds each stick by the thumb and the tips of the fingers. Loose wrists are needed to make graceful gestures.

Hula ʻUlīʻulī
feather-gourd-rattle dance

For the *hula ʻulīʻulī* (gourd rattle, containing seeds, with colored feathers at the top) the top of the handle just under the brightly colored feathers is held loosely between the thumb and fingers of the right hand. With a loose wrist the dancer shakes the gourd, which is partially filled with tiny pebbles or seeds, and taps it lightly against the palm of the free left hand, on the lap and on the shoulder.

Hula Pū'ili
split-bamboo dance

For the *hula pū'ili* (bamboo rattles) the dancer holds the closed end of the bamboo for a handle. With a loose wrist he rattles the long narrow strips by striking the split end against the hand, shoulder and mat.

'A'ohe i Pau ka 'Ike i Kāu Hālau
Not All Knowledge is Taught in Your School

words: traditional music: Moses Crabbe

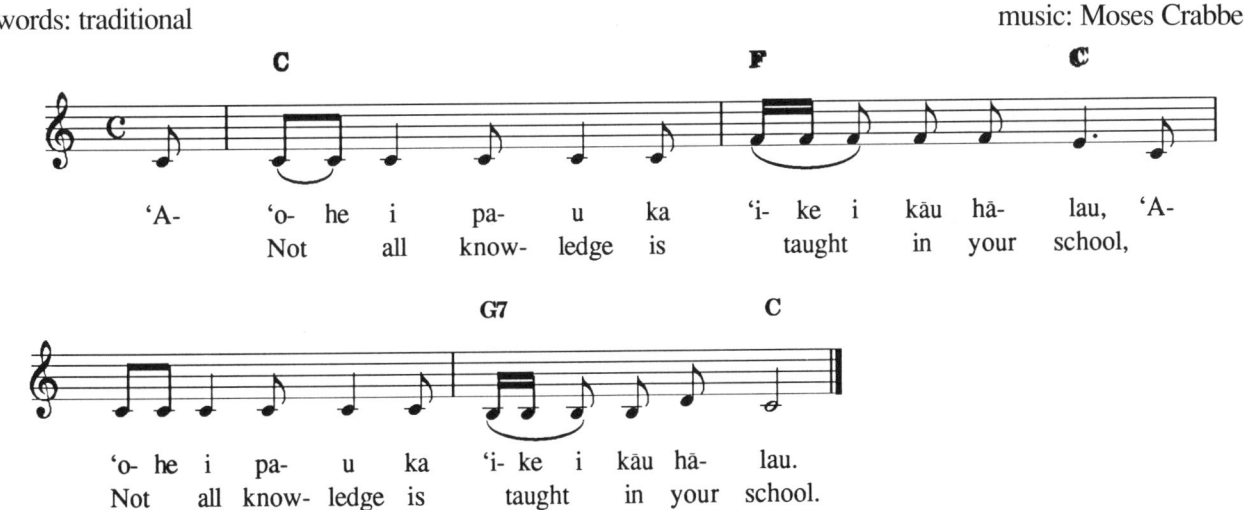

'A-'o-he i pa-u ka 'i-ke i kāu hā-lau, 'A-'o-he i pa-u ka 'i-ke i kāu hā-lau.
Not all know-ledge is taught in your school, Not all know-ledge is taught in your school.

Ka Wahine Noho Pono

words: Robin Makua

'Auhea 'oe e ka lani nui,	Where are you, princess of high rank,
Ka wahine kau i ka wēkiu.	Oh woman set on the highest summit.
Mahalo mākou i ka nani,	We appreciate the beauty,
O ka pua loke i milimili ai.	Of the rose that you so cherished.
Ke pua maila nō mākou,	We appear and blossom forth,
I ka wewehi o Kaiona.	In the glory of Kaiona.
E 'imi na'auao nei mākou,	We seek to gain knowledge,
Me 'oe e ka wahine noho pono.	Through you, oh virtuous woman.
E ola mau e ka lani ali'i,	Long live the heavenly princess,
'O Pauahi lani nui he inoa.	Whose royal name is Pauahi.

hula kahiko
(ancient *hula*)

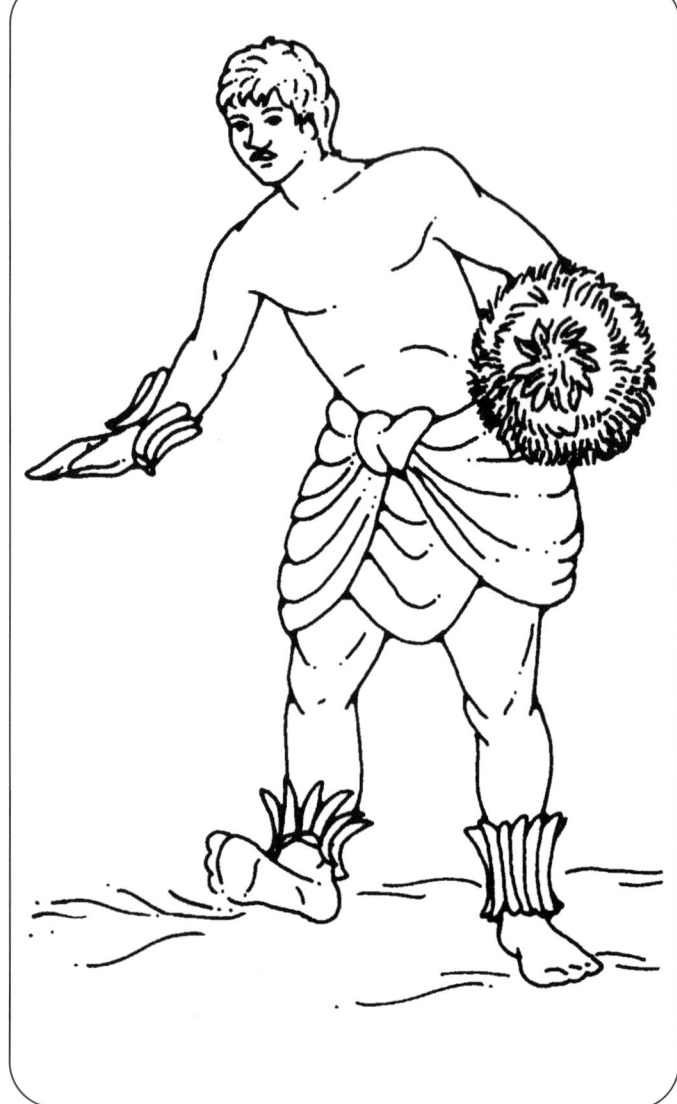

hula ʻauana
(modern *hula*)

Nā Hana Noʻeau
Crafts

Imagine not having stores—no places to purchase food, household goods and appliances, games and the other things we need to enjoy life as well as survive. Hawaiians of old lived in just such an environment. They were extremely self-sufficient, skillful in using natural materials to create all the things needed in their daily lives.

The expert craftsperson of old Hawaiʻi had devoted many years in training under the guidance of a master. Learning was done in the traditional manner through quiet observation and careful listening—followed by lengthy practice. Hawaiians were trained in great powers of memory, aiding the learning process. Having no writing system they relied on oral tradition.

Today we can still appreciate the high level of skill shown in the excellent craftswork of the early Hawaiians. These crafts included the construction of canoes and related fishing equipment, featherwork on such symbols of the *aliʻi* (chiefs or rulers) as capes and helmets, wooden bowls, gourd bowls, baskets plaited from vine rootlets, musical instruments and the finest *kapa* (tapa, or bark cloth) of all the Pacific cultures.

Ipu
bottle gourds

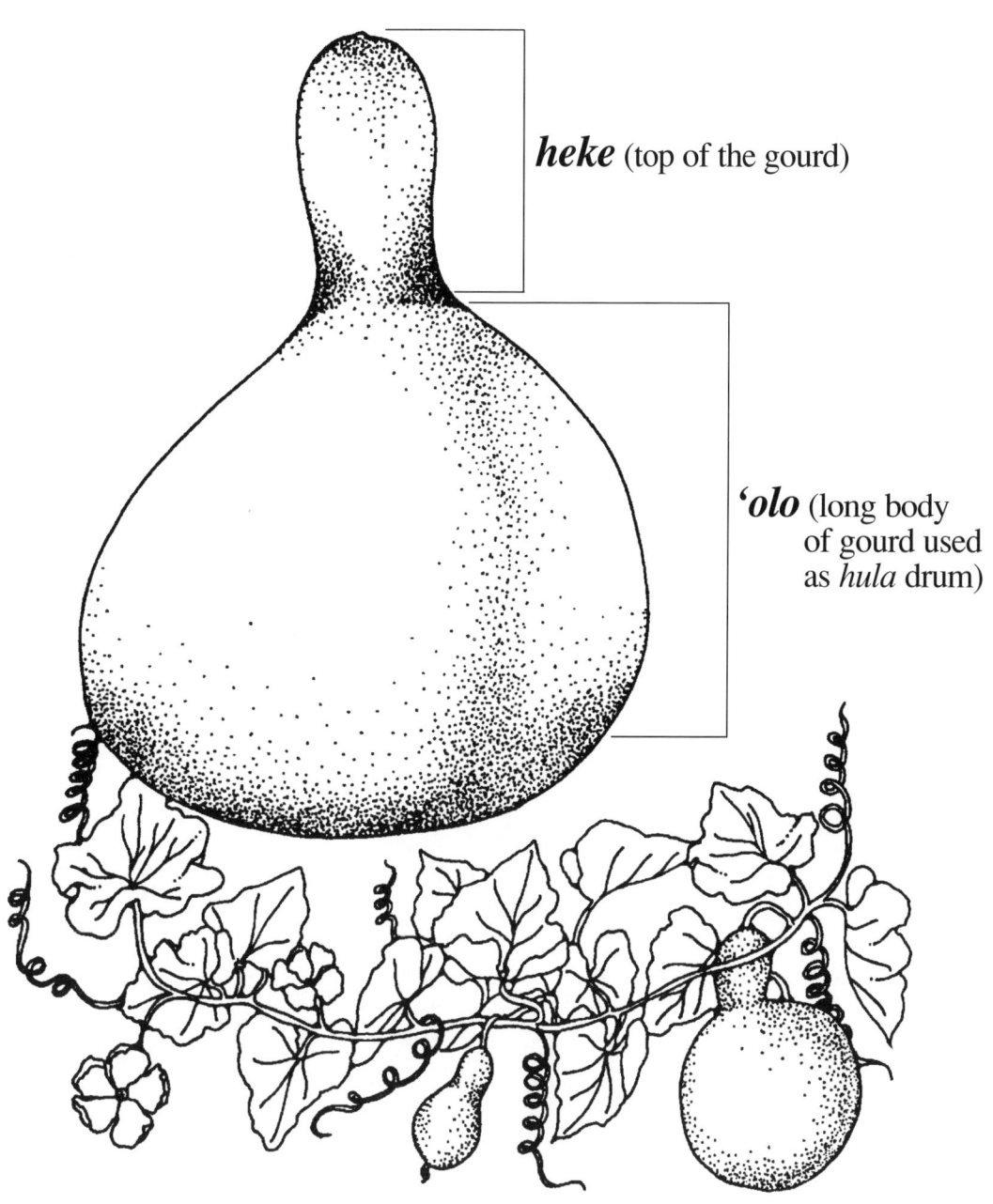

Ipu

Hawaiian planters grew a great number of gourds in a variety of shapes and sizes. Gourds were used in many different ways.

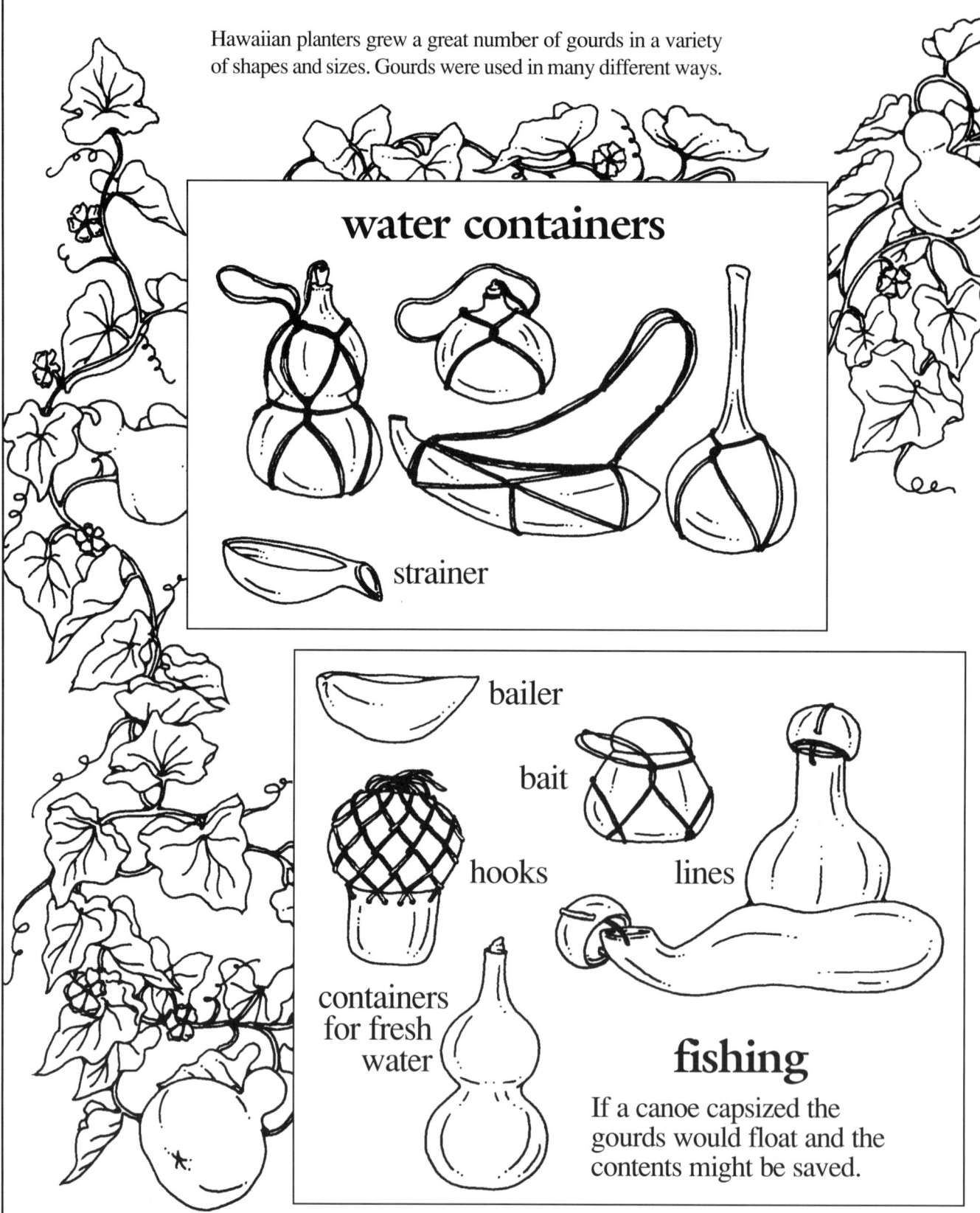

water containers

strainer

bailer

bait

hooks

lines

containers for fresh water

fishing

If a canoe capsized the gourds would float and the contents might be saved.

mask or helmet

baskets

closely twined around a selected gourd

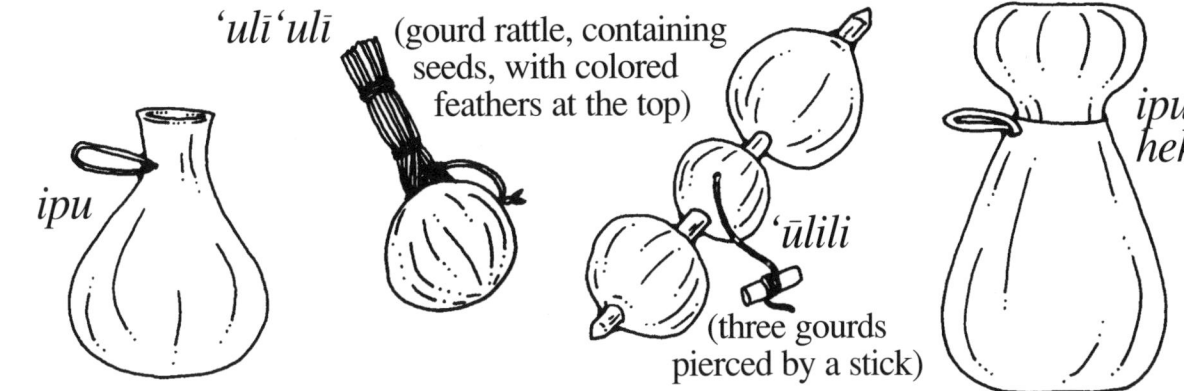

ipu

'ulī'ulī (gourd rattle, containing seeds, with colored feathers at the top)

'ūlili (three gourds pierced by a stick)

ipu heke

containers for storage and transporting

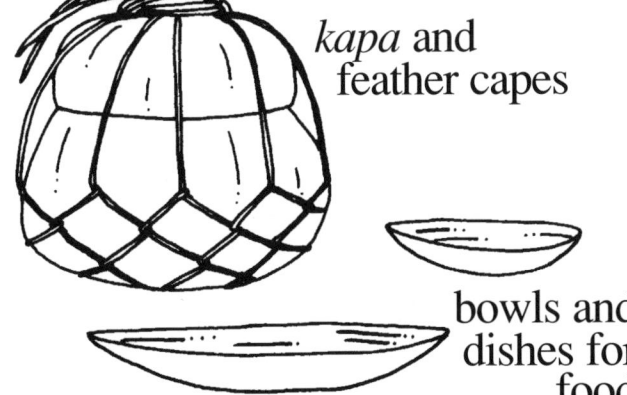

kapa and feather capes

bowls and dishes for food

cup

musical instruments

 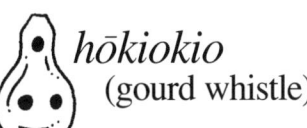

hōkiokio (gourd whistle)

oeoe (roarer)

89

Ipu Hula
gourd drum

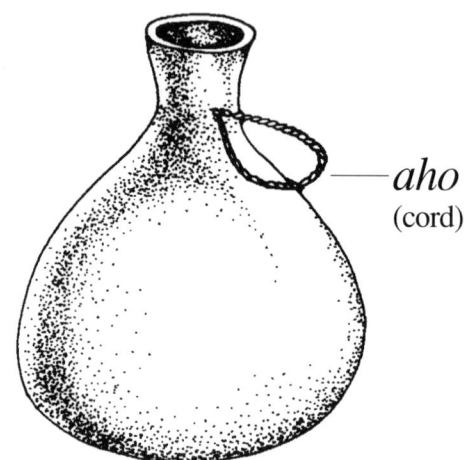
aho (cord)

materials needed:

1. *ipu*
2. tub for soaking
3. hacksaw
4. scouring pad
5. pump drill
6. long-handled spoon
7. cordage
8. *kukui* (candlenut) nut oil (or other kind of sealing oil)

procedure:

1. Soak the gourd in water for a few minutes to soften the outside dirt.
2. Scrub the outside with a scouring pad or coconut husk.
3. Cut off the *heke* (top).
4. Scrape the inside with a long-handled spoon. Soak the inside if it is difficult to clean out. This will soften the inside "meat" and make it easier to take out.
5. Dry the gourd.
6. Drill one hole in the neck of the *ipu*.
7. Attach cordage. (Make your own cordage from *hau* or coconut fibers or use any suitable commercial string.)
8. Rub the outside with *kukui* nut oil.

Ipu Kanu
gourd planter

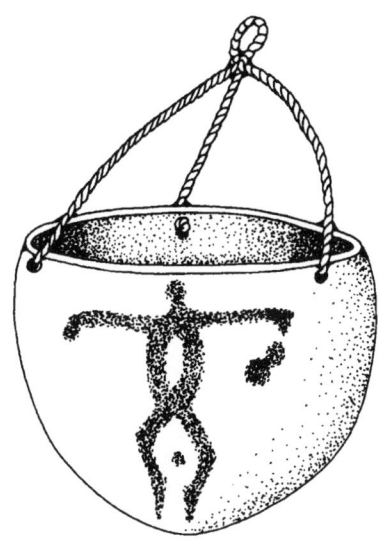

materials needed:

1. *heke*
2. tub for soaking
3. hacksaw
4. scouring pad
5. pump drill
6. long-handled spoon
7. cordage
8. marking pens
9. clear acrylic spray

procedure:

1. Scrape the inside of the *heke* you earlier sawed off the gourd.
2. Clean the outside of the *heke*.
3. Decorate with petroglyphs and *kapa* designs.
4. Spray lightly once or twice with acrylic spray.
5. Drill three *puka* (holes) near the opening.
6. Tie a cord in each *puka* and join them at the top to make a hanger for your planter.

Nā Kiʻi Pōhaku
petroglyphs

Nā 'Āpi'i
tapa-beater designs

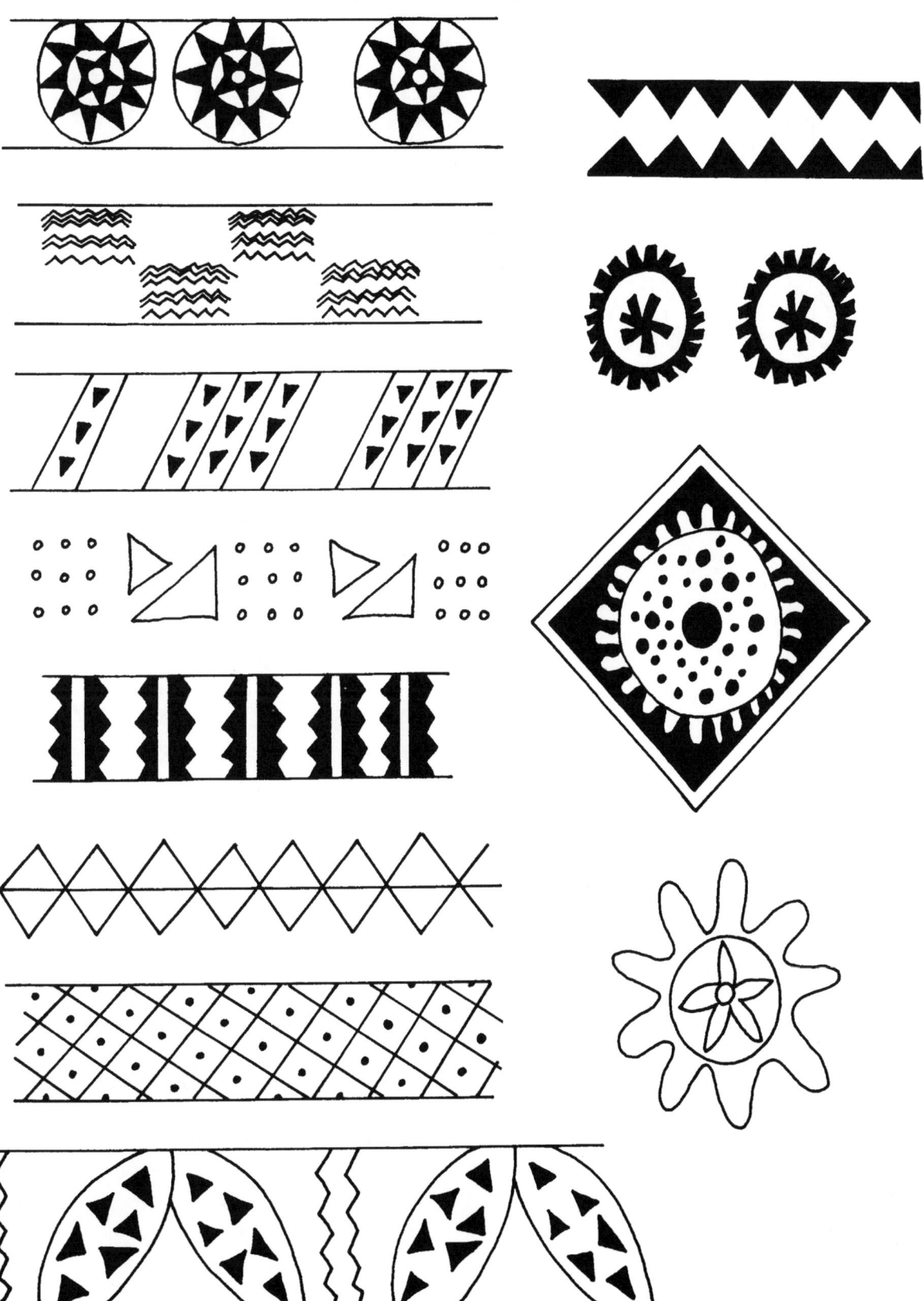

Ka ʻOhe Hano Ihu
the nose flute

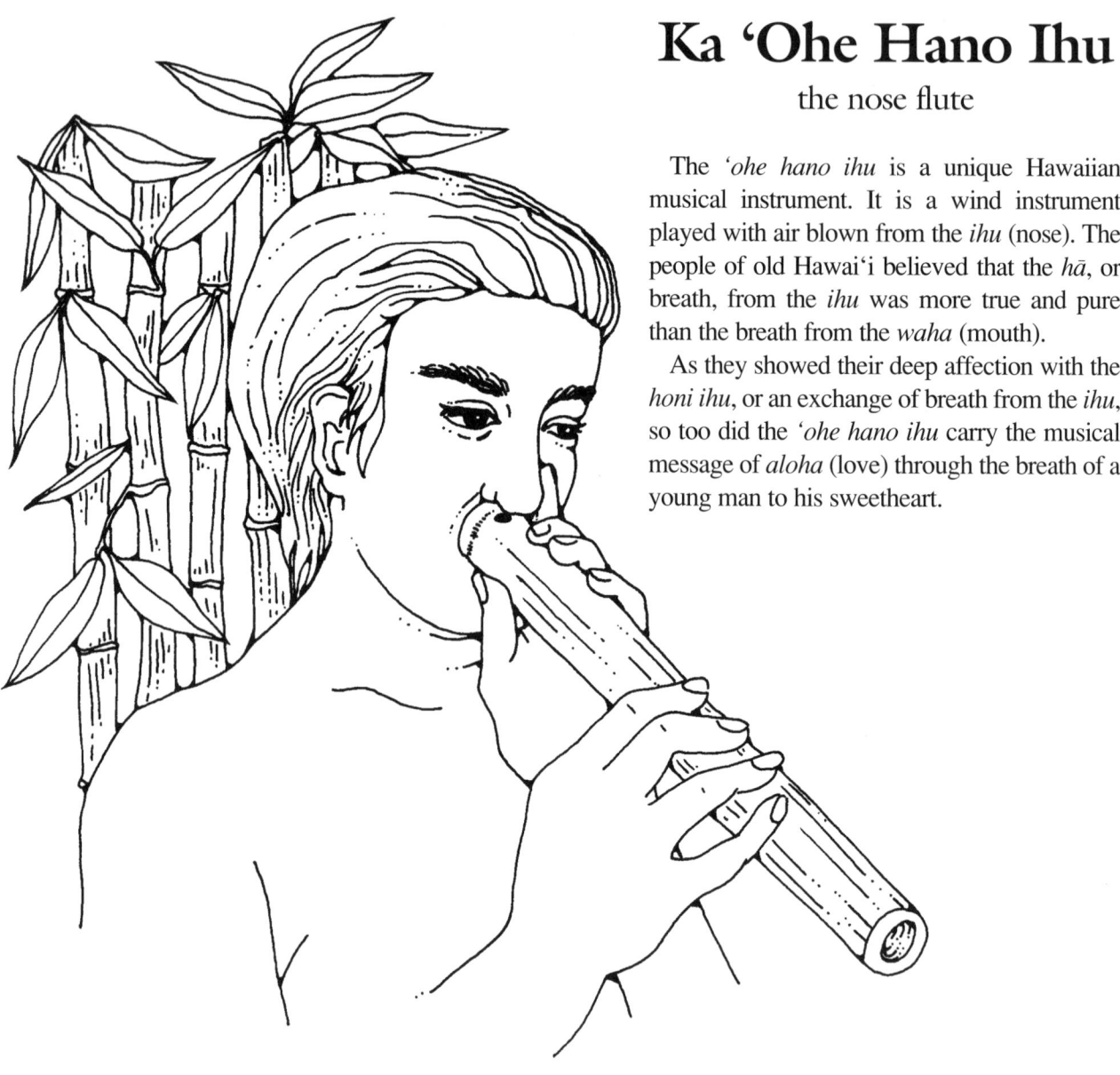

The ʻohe hano ihu is a unique Hawaiian musical instrument. It is a wind instrument played with air blown from the *ihu* (nose). The people of old Hawaiʻi believed that the *hā*, or breath, from the *ihu* was more true and pure than the breath from the *waha* (mouth).

As they showed their deep affection with the *honi ihu*, or an exchange of breath from the *ihu*, so too did the ʻohe hano ihu carry the musical message of *aloha* (love) through the breath of a young man to his sweetheart.

The ʻohe hano ihu is made of a length of *ʻohe* (bamboo) with one end closed by a node. A *puka* is made in the side as close to the node as possible. This is the *puka ihu* for the nose. About halfway down the length of bamboo, two or three more *puka* are made. These *puka manamana lima* are covered and uncovered by the fingers. By doing this different musical notes can be produced. Since Hawaiian music consists of chants with only a few different tones the two or three *puka manamana lima* are all that are necessary.

To play your ʻohe hano ihu close your left nostril with your index finger and place the *puka ihu* directly below the right nostril. Do not cover the *puka* but blow softly over it. It is very important to direct your air flow properly. You may have to adjust the position of the ʻohe hano ihu to find the proper angle.

Nānā I Ka Lā

Chant: Mahela Rosehill

♩ = 96 Larghetto

Nā-nā i ka lā, 'U-la nō, Ai-a ka lā, ma 'ō, "Kau ka lā i ka lo-lo," hu-la-li, hu-la-li, 'O ka lā, ka lā, ka lā, ka lā.

Hū
kukui top

tools and materials:

1. *kukui* nut
2. sandpaper or file
3. drill
4. coconut-leaf midrib

procedure:

1. Select a sturdy *kukui* nut. (Discard any which float when placed in water.)
2. With sandpaper or file flatten the top of the nut to make it easier to drill.
3. Drill a hole in the top of the nut.
4. Fit the peg of coconut-leaf midrib securely in hole.

to play:

Hold the coconut-leaf midrib between your thumb and index finger. Spin the top with a finger-snapping motion. Challenge a classmate.

Kamani Pendant

tools and materials:

1. *kamani* (a large tree, *Colophyllum inophyllum*) nut
2. sharp paring or pocket knife
3. coarse, medium and fine sandpaper
4. drill (electric or hand)
5. metal tweezers
6. jewelry findings (pin, 2 rosettes, slip ring)
7. clear acrylic spray

procedure:

1. Remove the outer skin of the nut with the knife.
2. Using coarse sandpaper remove all white particles of the outer skin.
3. Continue sanding with medium and then with fine sandpaper.
4. Drill a hole through the nut.
5. Select a pin, two rosettes (one for the top and one for the bottom) and a slip ring.
6. String in this order: pin, rosette, *kamani* nut, rosette.
7. Trim off the excess length of the pin and use tweezers to twist a loop in the top of the pin above the rosette.
8. Insert slip ring into loop and twist loop closed.
9. Spray with clear acrylic spray.

Methods of Making Lei

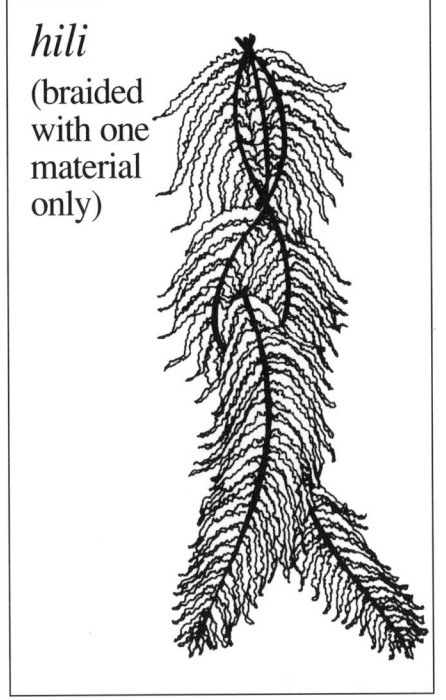

hili
(braided with one material only)

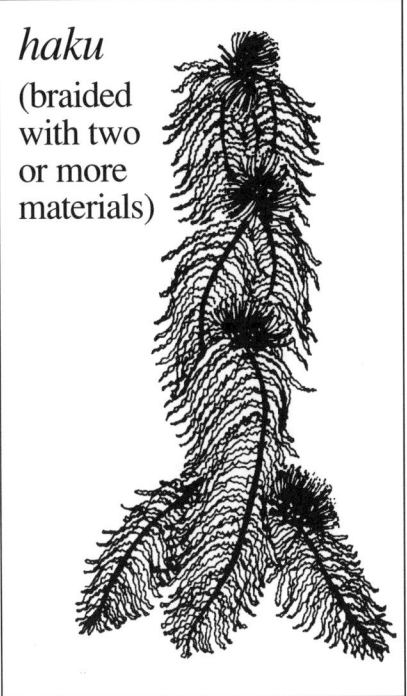

haku
(braided with two or more materials)

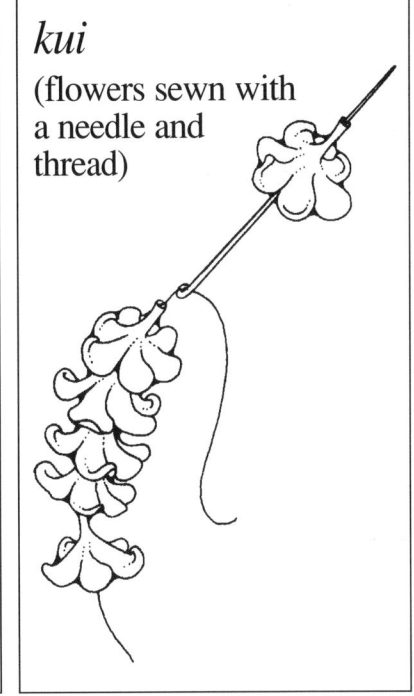

kui
(flowers sewn with a needle and thread)

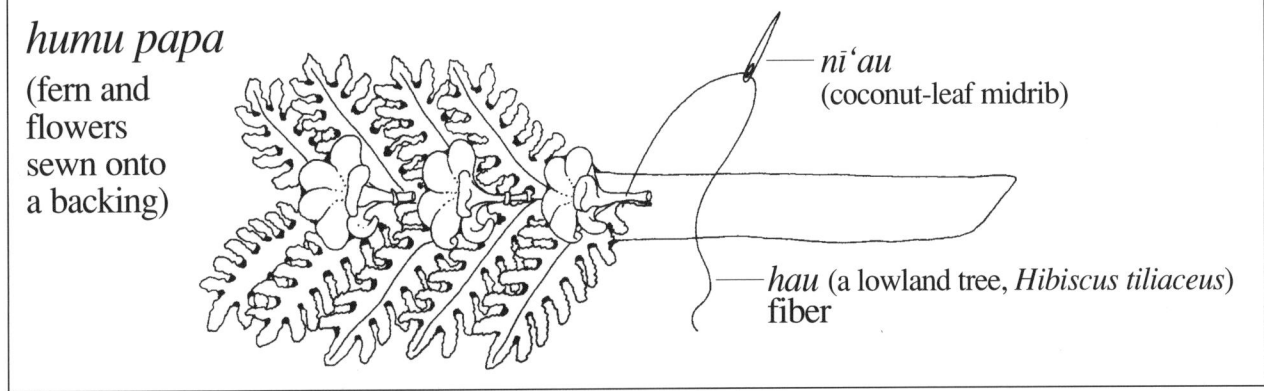

humu papa
(fern and flowers sewn onto a backing)

nī'au (coconut-leaf midrib)

hau (a lowland tree, *Hibiscus tiliaceus*) fiber

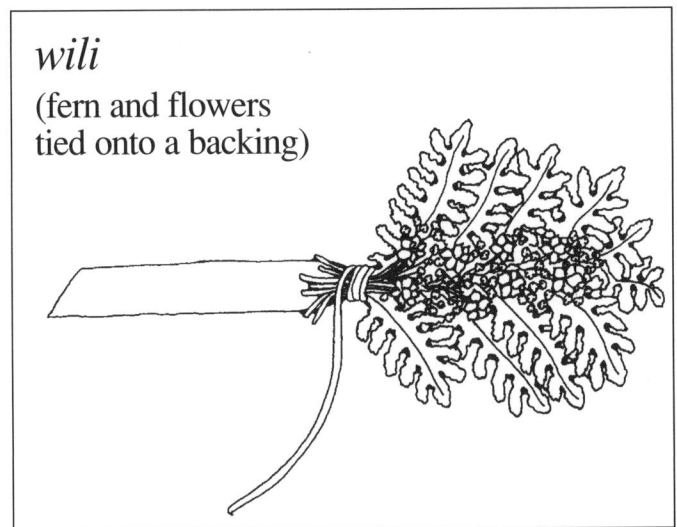

wili
(fern and flowers tied onto a backing)

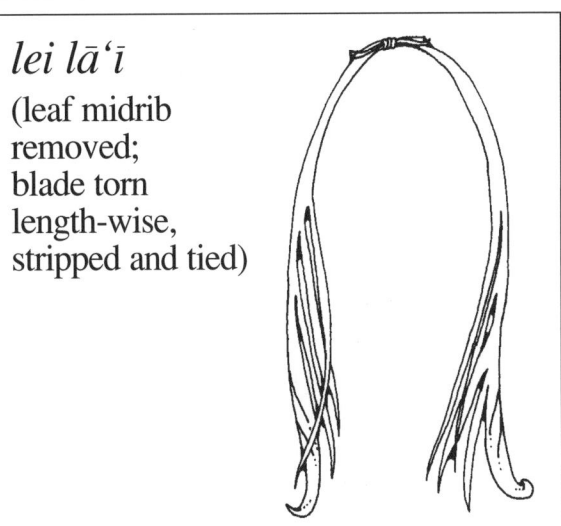

lei lā'ī
(leaf midrib removed; blade torn length-wise, stripped and tied)

Pala‘ie
loop and ball game

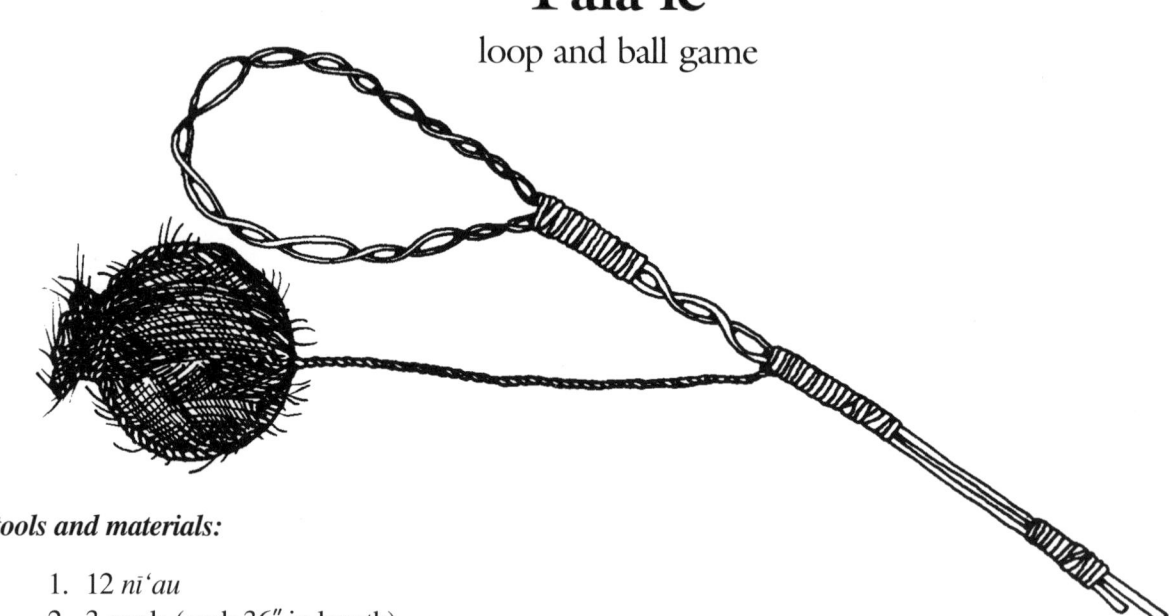

tools and materials:

1. 12 *nī‘au*
2. 3 cords (each 36″ in length)
3. palm cloth or *kapa* paper
4. scissors
5. upholsterer's needle

procedure:

1. Select twelve mature, firm, freshly cut *nī‘au*, or coconut-leaf midribs, from leaves 28″ or longer if possible.
2. Gather these into a tight bundle and wind a strong cord firmly around the base at least twelve times and knot securely.
3. Braid the *nī‘au* from the base to the tip in a three-ply braid producing a flat, firm handle for the *pala‘ie*.
4. Make a loop from the braided tip, using the portion far enough from the tip to form a firm loop which will not bend under the weight of the ball. The loop should be an approximately 3″ x 4″ oval. Tie the tip to the handle with twelve or more turns of cord and trim the free ends of the *nī‘au*.
5. Make a ball of *‘a‘a* (palm cloth). The *‘a‘a* forms at the base of the *‘a‘a niu* (coconut leaf). A superior cloth, *‘a‘a loulu*, comes from the *loulu* (fan palm). Use *kapa* paper if palm cloth is not available. To make the ball take a sheet of *‘a‘a* at least a foot square, place a very few fragments of the same material in the center as stuffing, then lift up the edges to form a ball about 3″– 4″ in diameter. It must be slightly larger than the loop of the *pala‘ie* and light in weight.
6. Close the ball by tying it with one end of a cord about a yard long. Use a heavy needle and draw the loose end of the cord through the center of the ball and out the side opposite the tie. This allows the ball to swing with proper balance. Make a needle from a sliver of bamboo if an upholsterer's needle is not available.
7. Attach the free end of the cord to the handle of the *pala‘ie*. Note that the loop of the *pala‘ie* is not centered but curves to one side. A right-handed player holds the handle so that the loop is toward the left. The string which carries the ball should be secured so that it comes out from the left side of the handle and is just long enough to allow the ball to reach the center of the loop.

"Why the Mullet Swim Around Oʻahu"

Word List

ʻamaʻama ....mullet
    (note: there are different names for different stages of growth)
iʻa kaulaʻi ....salt fish, dried fish
kai ....sea
kō ....sugar cane
limu ....seaweed
mahiʻai ....farmer
maiʻa ....bananas
nā lawaiʻa ....fishermen
pipipi ....general name for small shellfish
ʻuala ....sweet potatoes

Why the Mullet Swim Around O‘ahu

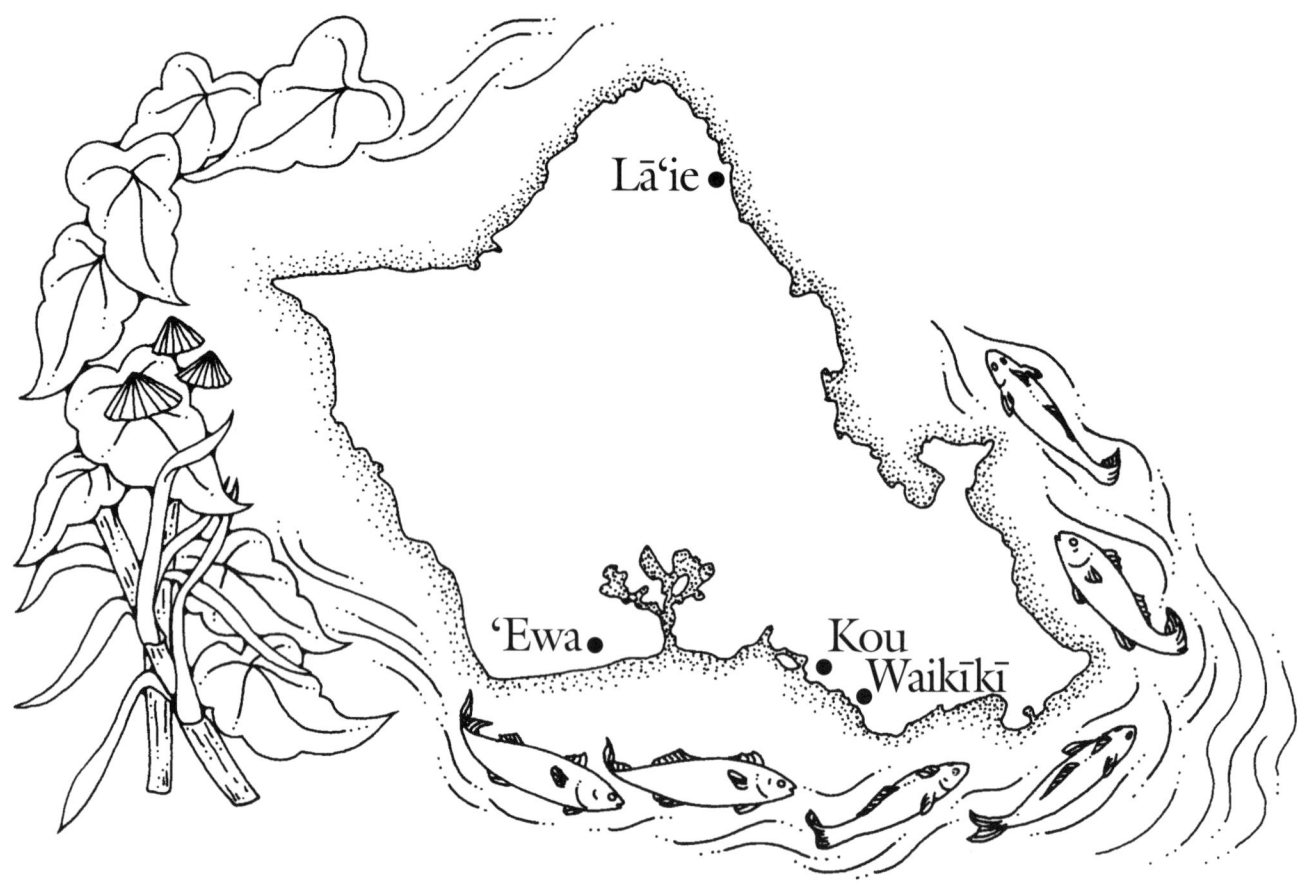

Each year the **mullet** swim from ‘Ewa past Waikīkī, around the end of O‘ahu, as far as Lā‘ie. Then they swim back. "Why do they do this?" people wondered, and told this story to explain.

A young woman of ‘Ewa had angered her family and had been sent away. She walked for many days, welcomed by strangers, yet longing for her home. At last she met a young **farmer**. Love grew between these two, they were married and built a home at Lā‘ie. There the young man made a fine *kalo* patch, with **sugar cane** and **bananas** on its banks. He also had good **sweet potatoes**. With **shellfish** and **seaweed** from the reef his family was well fed, but still they longed for **fish**. "The **sea** here at Lā‘ie is empty," said the man, "and every day I think how good some **fish** would taste!"

"Yes," his wife answered. "At my childhood home in ‘Ewa there were **fish** in plenty. Why don't you go there and get some for us?"

"Bring **fish** from ‘Ewa!" the husband said. "Fresh **fish** would spoil! And a backload of dried **fish** would grow very heavy through many days of walking."

"Bring **fish** in the **sea**," answered his wife.

"**Fish** in the **sea**? I do not understand."

"My father is a man of wisdom," the young woman said. "He has power from the gods. It may be my parents have forgotten their anger toward me and will welcome you. Then my father will offer you some gift. Ask him for **fish**. He will show you a well-filled store house and offer you **salt fish**. You must answer, 'I cannot carry such a heavy load. Give me **fish** in the **sea**.'"

The husband stared at his wife, puzzled. She smiled quietly. "Do as I say," she told him. "Then you will understand."

The young man trusted his wife and, though still puzzled, made the journey. It was a long, long journey following a trail beside the ocean. After many days he came to 'Ewa.

The wife's family had forgotten their anger and were eager for news of their daughter. They welcomed the young man and when they found he was their son-in-law they wailed for joy. He told of his wife, of their good lands and food plants.

"You two have prospered," said the father. "You have *kalo,* **sweet potatoes, bananas, sugar cane.** Is there anything you lack—any gift I can give my dear daughter and her husband?"

"We need **fish**," the young man answered. "Near Lā'ie there are none."

"You shall have **fish**," the father told him and led him to the store house. "Here are **salt fish**," he said. "Half of them are yours."

The young man remembered his wife's words. "How can I carry them so far?" he asked. "My back would break! Oh, give us **fish** in the **sea**."

"If my gods are willing," the father promised and went to pray.

The young man stayed in 'Ewa many days but nothing more was said about a gift. "I must return," he told the family. He was given a bundle of food for his journey, but nothing else.

"Take our *aloha* (love) to your wife," the parents said. Then, as the young man started, the father added, "You shall take **fish** in the **sea**."

As he walked the young man repeated the words, "**fish** in the **sea**." Over and over he said them, but he could not understand their meaning.

He spent a night in Kou, at the mouth of the Nuʻuanu Stream, and found men busy fishing. "There is a run of **mullet**," he was told. All the village feasted.

"I wish we had such **fish** at Lāʻie," said the traveler. "Our **sea** is empty."

Next day he paused at Waikīkī. There too men were busy fishing. "There is a run of **mullet**," he was told.

He journeyed on. At every stop he heard of **fish** and always envied the **fishermen**. "At Lāʻie the **sea** is empty," he repeated many times.

At last he reached his home. His wife welcomed him gladly. He told her of her parents and of his journey. "Everywhere there were **fish**," he said. "Only here the **sea** is empty." His wife smiled wisely.

Next morning she woke him at sunrise. "They have come!" she said. "The **mullet**."

He hurried out. It was true! The bay was red with **mullet**. "How strange!" he said. "The **sea** is no longer empty!"

"These are the **fish** you brought," answered his wife. "My father prayed and the gods sent the **mullet** to follow you."

The young man hurried to join his neighbors in fishing. So that was it! At Kou, at Waikīkī, everywhere along his journey men had caught **fish** because the **mullet** followed him! The young man thanked the gods.

From a Hawaiian newspaper,
translated by
Mary Kawena Pūkuʻi

Nā Manu o Hawaiʻi Kahiko
birds of old Hawaiʻi

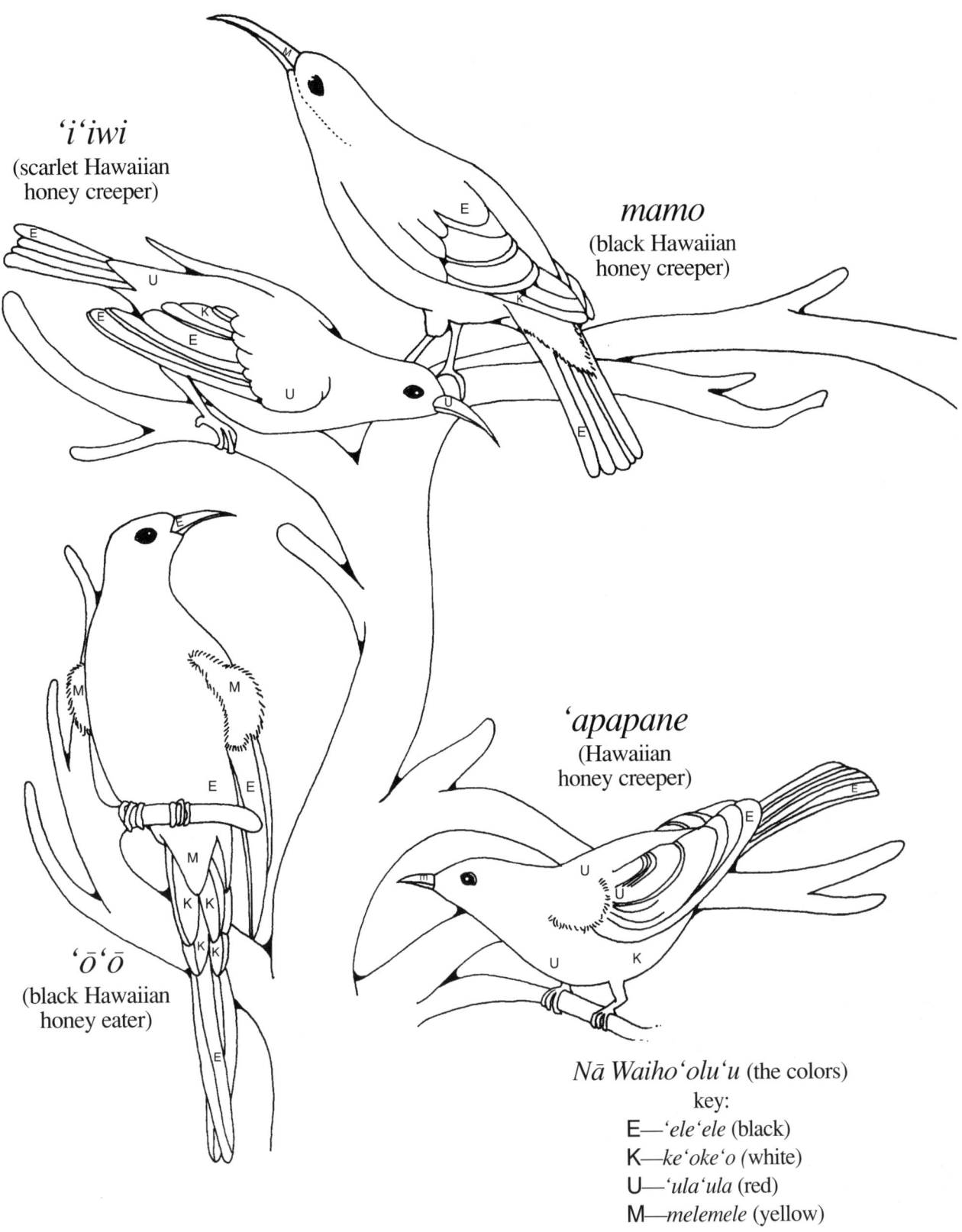

ʻiʻiwi
(scarlet Hawaiian honey creeper)

mamo
(black Hawaiian honey creeper)

ʻapapane
(Hawaiian honey creeper)

ʻōʻō
(black Hawaiian honey eater)

Nā Waihoʻoluʻu (the colors)
key:
E—*eleʻele* (black)
K—*keʻokeʻo* (white)
U—*ʻulaʻula* (red)
M—*melemele* (yellow)

pueo (Hawaiian short-eared owl)

'io (Hawaiian hawk)

'elepaio (flycatcher)

Nā Waihoʻoluʻu (the colors) key:
E—*eleʻele* (black)
U—*ulaʻula* (red)
M—*melemele* (yellow)

Pauahi's Cape

Professional bird hunters studied the habits and roosting places of birds. Some hunters would put a sticky substance on the tree branches where they thought the birds they wanted would come. When the birds landed their feet would stick to the branches. The men would take hold of each bird and pull out the feathers they wanted. Then they would wipe the birds' claws clean with *kukui* nut oil and let the birds go free. Nets, snares or long poles with twine loops on the end were also used for catching birds. The beautiful feathers were used to make capes, cloaks, helmets, *lei* and images of gods.

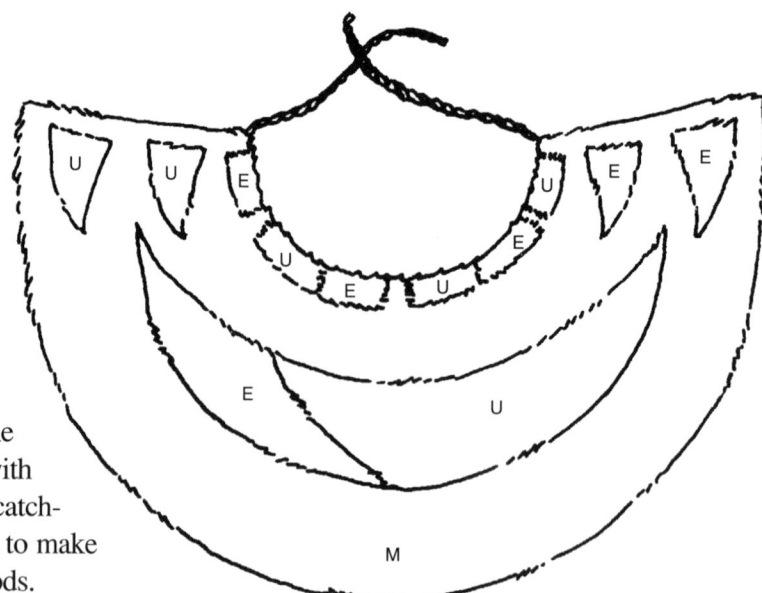

Nā Meakanu Hawaiʻi

Hawaiian Plants

Hawaiʻi is by nature a favored place for agriculture. The sunny tropical climate, good soil and abundant water encourage plant growth all year.

Polynesian settlers brought with them their principal food crops, other useful plants and a knowledge of their proper care. They lived along the shoreline, preferably at the entrance to valleys. Here the streams furnished fresh water for farming and the ocean an abundant supply of fish.

The planters grew most of their food in the rich soil of the valleys and on the lower slopes of the hills. They knew the type of soil in which each plant thrived and its preference for sun and moisture.

Plants brought here by the Polynesians included those used for food, building materials, clothing, cordage, utensils and medicines. These were shared equally without greed or selfishness.

While at Hoʻomākaʻikaʻi you will have the opportunity to learn the names and uses of several plants found only in Hawaiʻi. In addition you will gain "hands-on" experience in working with plants. This opportunity will further your understanding of the traditions and culture of early Hawaiians and their relationship with the natural environment.

Kalo

Kalo

There were 275 to 300 varieties of *kalo* (taro) known to the early Hawaiians.

Medicine

The stem of the raw leaf was rubbed on insect bites to relieve pain and to prevent swelling. Raw rootstock was rubbed on wounds to stop bleeding. Mashed *poi* (cooked taro corms, rarely breadfruit, pounded and thinned with water) was used as a poultice or bandage on infected sores.

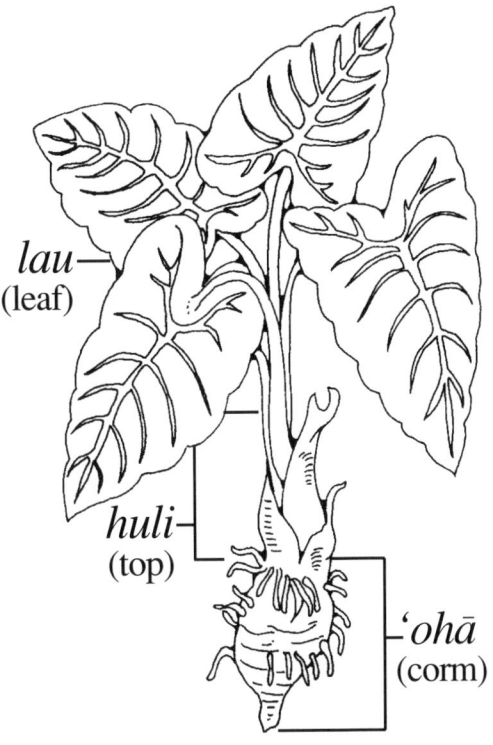

lau (leaf)

huli (top)

'ohā (corm)

Paste

Poi was used as paste to glue pieces of *kapa* (tapa) together.

Fishing

Grated raw corm was used as bait for fish such as *'ōpelu* (mackerel scad).

Dye

Juice from the *poni* (purple) variety produced a rich red dye used for dyeing *kapa*. Seven other varieties were also used for dyes.

Food

The *kalo* corm was cooked in an *imu* (underground oven) then peeled and eaten. *Poi*, the Hawaiian's most important starchy food, was made from the cooked, peeled and pounded corm. It was first mashed into a thick paste called *pa'i'ai*. When water was added the thinner paste was called *poi*. The cooked corm was also sliced and dried for use as food on long voyages.

Kūlolo is a pudding made by cooking grated raw corm, grated coconut meat and coconut milk. Young leaves called *lū'au* were cooked with pork in the imu or wrapped in *kī* (ti) leaves for a dish called *laulau*. Leaf stems were peeled and cooked for greens. Corm was also used to feed and fatten pigs.

Huki I Ke Kalo

words and music: unknown

Huki i ke kalo	Pull the taro
Huki, huki mai.	
Ku'i i ke kalo	Pound the taro
Ku'i, ku'i mai.	
'Ai i ke kalo	Eat the taro
Mā'ona mai	
Mm—mm—mm	

Kukui

The green husk of the *kukui* (candlenut) fruit was pounded with water to make a pale gray dye. Ashes from burned nuts were made into a black dye for tattooing, for painting the hulls of canoes and for *kapa*.

The inner bark of the tree was pounded with water to make reddish-brown dye for fish nets and *kapa*.

Oil from the kernels was used as a decorative and waterproofing finish for surfboards.

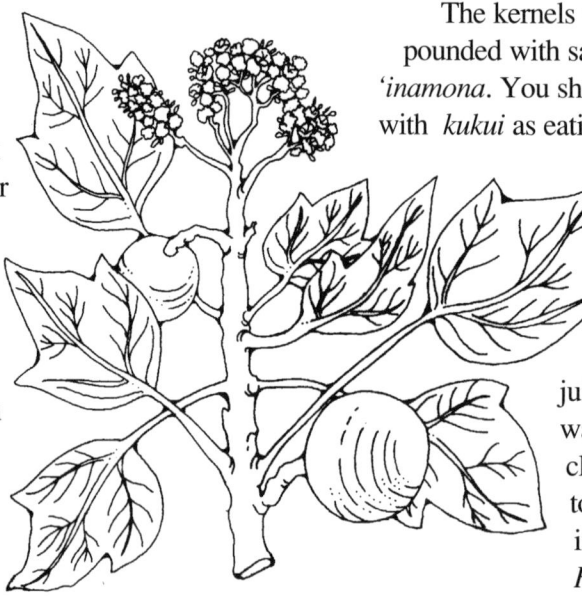

Food

The kernels were roasted, shelled and pounded with salt to make relish called *'inamona*. You should be extremely careful with *kukui* as eating raw kernels can make a person very sick.

Fishing

Roasted kernels were chewed by fishermen and the juice was spat over the water to make it smooth and clear. The wood was used to make floats for fish nets if *hau* (a lowland tree, *Hibiscus tiliaceus*) wood was not available.

Medicine

Sap from the green fruit was rubbed in children's mouths to treat *'ea* (thrush—white spots in the mouth). A mixture of the flowers and *'uala* (sweet potatoes) was also eaten to treat *'ea*. The sap was used to treat open skin wounds for faster healing. Leaves were used as bandages for swellings and infections.

Lei

The hard shells of nuts were polished and strung into *lei* (garlands or wreaths).

Ihoiho Kukui

Ihoiho kukui (*kukui*-nut candles) were formed by stringing roasted or dried kernels on short coconut midribs or splinters of bamboo. They were placed in a stone bowl filled with sand. Each kernel burned for two-to-three minutes.

Illumination

The nut kernels were important as light sources because of the high quality and large quantity of oil they contained.

Lama Kū

Large torches were made by stringing kernels on several midribs wrapped in *lā'ī* (dried *kī* leaf). These torches were then placed at the tips of bamboo handles.

Poho Kukui

Lamps were made from stone bowls filled with *kukui* nut oil. Twisted strips of *kapa* were used as wicks.

Lama

Small torches were made by stuffing hollow bamboo poles with roasted kernels.

Mai‘a

More than seventy varieties of *mai‘a* (bananas and plantains) were known to the early Hawaiians.

Fruit

Depending on the variety the fruit was eaten raw or cooked. When *kalo* was scarce bananas were mashed to make a food similar to *poi*.

Dye

A dye was made from the juice of the flower buds.

Trunk

Trunks from banana and plantain trees were used as rollers to move large canoes. They were also crushed and placed in *imu* to create steam as well as being used as targets for spear practice.

Leaves

The leaves were used to cover food placed in the *imu*. They were also used to make temporary sandals.

Medicine

Honey secretions from the tips of flowers were fed to babies for extra nourishment. Juice from the roots of certain varieties was used to treat *‘ea*.

Religion

Leaves sometimes used to cover *unu* (small religious altars). Fruit was used for offerings to various gods. After death the bodies of *ali‘i* were wrapped in the leaves.

‘Uala

About two hundred thirty varieties of *‘uala* (sweet potatoes) were grown in early Hawai‘i.

Kamapua‘a was known as the god of the sweet potato.

Food

The tubers or roots were baked in *imu* and eaten. Sweet potatoes were also baked, peeled, mashed and mixed with water to make a food similar to *poi*.

For dessert grated tubers were mixed with coconut milk, wrapped in *lā‘ī* and baked. Tender young leaves were cooked and eaten as a green vegetable. The tubers were also used to make a fermented drink.

Flooring

Old vines and leaves were used as padding under floor mats.

Medicine

Certain varieties of *‘uala* were eaten to induce vomiting and as an asthma cure. Some were also used as a laxative, a gargle to clear the throat of phlegm and in various other medicinal mixtures.

Hog Food

Vines, leaves, inferior tubers and peelings were used for the final fattening of pigs.

ʻUlu

Fruit
ʻUlu (breadfruit) was baked in an *imu* and sometimes made into *poi* or used for pudding. It is considered a good source of starch and vitamin B. It was also used to fatten pigs.

Trunk
The wood was used to make *pahu* (drums), *poi*-pounding boards, for woodwork in houses and canoe bows and stem pieces. Because of its lightness the wood was also used to make surfboards.

Sheath of Male Flower
This covering of the flower was used as sandpaper in final smoothing of utensils and in polishing bowls and *kukui* nuts.

Dye
Young male flowers make a tan dye. Older ones make a brown dye.

Medicine
Thickened dried sap was used for certain skin diseases. Leaf buds were used for the cure of *ʻea*.

Latex
Chewing gum was made from solidified milky sap. The thick sap was also used as a glue for joining two gourds to make a drum, as caulking to fill canoe seams and to catch birds so their feathers could be removed to be used for decoration and clothing.

Kō

Early Hawaiians cultivated over forty different varieties of *kō* (sugar cane).

Food
The stalk was chewed as a sweet food between meals and carried on long journeys and chewed for quick energy. The juice was fed to babies and used to sweeten desserts like *haupia* (cornstarch, formerly arrowroot, and coconut cream pudding) and *kūlolo* (*kalo* and coconut cream pudding).

Leaves
If *pili* grass (*Heteropogon contortus*) was scarce *kō* leaves were often used to thatch houses or as a covering for inside walls.

Medicine
Stalks were used to sweeten medicine or chewed after taking medicine. They were considered an ingredient for some medicinal mixtures.

Kī

Clothing
Kī leaves were used to make garments such as rain capes, *hula* (Hawaiian dance) skirts (a style which was not of Hawaiian origin but was brought from Kiribati, sometimes referred to as the Gilbert Islands) and sandals.

Fishing
Leaves were used to wrap bait to catch sharks. In the *hukilau* (net fishing) leaf fronds were shaken to frighten the fish towards the drag nets. A lure used to catch *heʻe* (octopus, commonly called "squid" in Hawaiʻi) was a stick with a hook, a stone and tuft of *lāʻī*.

Religion
The plant was sacred to the god Lono. When leaves of the plant were worn around the neck of the *kahuna* (priest) it was a sign of high rank or divine power. It was used to ward off evil spirits. In war the leaves were carried into battle held straight up and dropped to signify surrender.

Stain
The juice from the pounded root was used to stain surfboards.

Thatching
Leaves were used for house roofs and sides. The temple for the god Lono was thatched with *kī*.

Medicine
Leaves dipped in cold spring water were placed on the forehead to relieve headache. Leaves wrapped around hot stones were used to soothe backaches or sore muscles. Young leaves were used as bandages for cuts.

Food Service
Leaves were used for wrapping *laulau* (wrapped pork, beef, fish or *kalo*, generally, to be baked or steamed) to hold food or wrap fish or meat for *lāwalu* (cooking fish or meat by binding them with *kī* leaves and grilling over coals) and placed in the *imu*. Leaves were also used to wrap and store *paʻi ʻai* (pounded undiluted *kalo*). Cut leaves were used as plates and cups. The root was baked in the *imu* and eaten like candy.

He Hana Pūʻolo
chant: Kaipo Hale

He aha ka hana?	*He hana pūʻolo!*
He aha ko loko?	*He ʻai ko loko!*
He ʻai wale nō?	*ʻAʻole paha!*
He aha hou aʻe?	*He mau lei nō hoʻi!*
He hana maʻalahi?	*ʻAe! ʻAe!*
He hana maikaʻi?	*ʻAe! ʻAe!*

Ua pau nō ia!

Koa

Koa trees (the largest native forest trees, *Acacia koa*) are usually found in drier forests on mountain sides.

- Generally at elevations between 1,500 and 4,000 feet but sometimes lower or higher.
- When grown close together, the tree trunks grow straight and as tall as 60 feet before beginning to branch out.
- What appear to be crescent-shaped "leaves" are actually flattened leaf stems that function as leaves. True leaves are small and oval-shaped and found mostly on young trees.

Trunk

The trunks of *koa* trees are used to make:
- canoe hulls • paddles • surfboards
- calabashes (but not used for food bowls because *koa* sap has a disagreeable flavor)

Tannin from the bark is used for tanning various animal skins.

Endemic

The *koa* tree is native to Hawai'i and is found nowhere else.

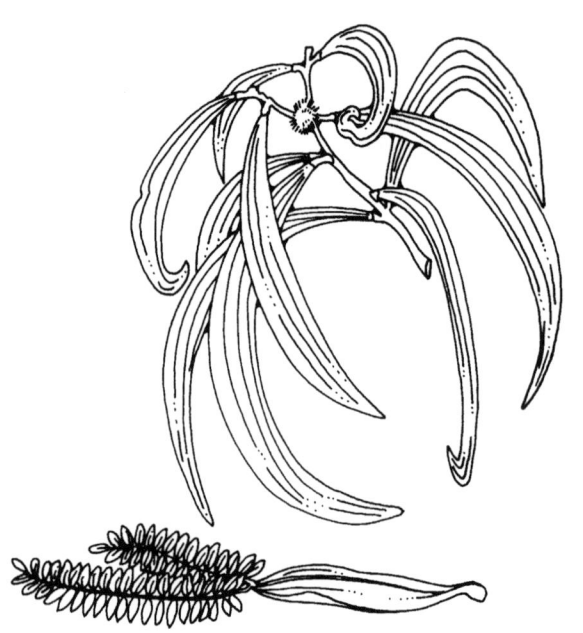

Pia

Starch was obtained from the *pia* (Polynesian arrowroot) tuber, which was the only part of the plant used.

Medicine

Raw starch was mixed in water and drunk as a treatment for diarrhea. When mixed with *'alaea* (red-colored, high-iron-content clay) it was considered a treatment for dysentery.

Food

The starch was mixed with coconut milk, wrapped in *lā'ī* and steamed in an *imu* to make a pudding called *haupia*. The recipe was brought to Hawai'i by Tahitians.

Hau

Branches

The slightly curved branches were used for canoe outrigger booms or outrigger floats if the lighter *wiliwili* (a leguminous tree, *Erythrina sandwicensis*) wood was not available.

Smaller branches were used for:
- adze handles
- massage sticks
- fire plows
- lightweight spears for battle practice
- fish net floats
- frames for kites

Medicine

The slimy sap under the bark at the base of the flower is used as a mild laxative. It was also given to women in labor to help speed delivery of their babies.

Inner Bark

This bark was twisted or braided into cordage for:
- support for water-holding gourds and to fasten covers of *lau hala* (pandanus leaf) baskets
- snapping line design onto *kapa*
- sewing *kapa* bed sheets together
- making nets when *olonā* (a native shrub related to *māmaki*) was scarce
- sandals
- ropes
- strings for bows
- slings

Hala

Male Flower

The leaves (bracts) of the *hala* (pandanus or screw pine) were used to make the finest garments. Pollen was used as a love charm and talcum.

Medicine

The tender tips of the aerial roots are rich in Vitamin B and were eaten raw or cooked for medicine.

Trunk

The male trees are hard through to the core and were used for posts and *'ūkēkē* (striking musical bows).

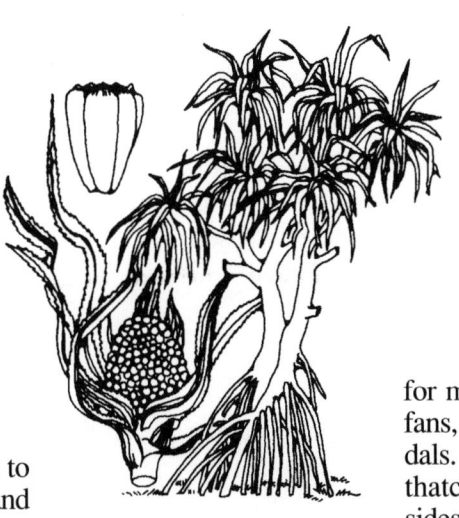

Fruit

The near-ripe fruit was cut and used to make *lei*. Older fruit were used for brushes. The nut-like centers of the mature keys (segments) were eaten in time of famine.

Lau Hala

The leaves were plaited for mats, canoe sails, baskets, fans, pillows, kites and sandals. They were also used for thatching house roofs and sides.

Olonā

Cordage

Fiber from the inner bark was twisted into a strong cordage for:
- fish nets and lines
- *kōkō* (nets used as carrying containers)
- net base for *lā'ī* rain capes, feather capes, cloaks and helmets
- tying adze heads to *hau* handles
- repairing cracks in gourd and calabash containers

Endemic

The *olonā* plant is native to Hawai'i and is found nowhere else.

Wauke

Kapa (tapa)

The inner bark of the *wauke* (paper mulberry) made the softest, finest and most durable *kapa* known. *Kapa* made from *wauke* was washable.

'Ōlena

'*Ōlena* is known elsewhere as turmeric. It is a member of the ginger family and is widely used as both a spice and a dye. Leaf stalks grow in the spring with yellow and white flowers rising from yellow roots, the flowers drop off in the fall.

Dye

Juice from the raw root makes yellow dye which was a favorite of many early Hawaiians. Juice from the cooked root makes deep orange dye. '*Ōlenalena* means "yellow" or "dye made from the '*ōlena* plant."

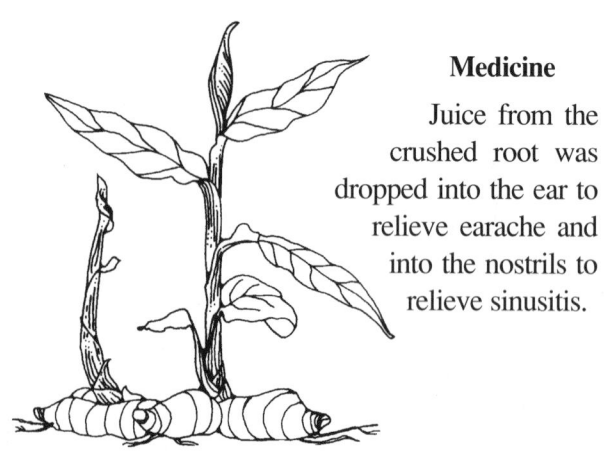

Medicine

Juice from the crushed root was dropped into the ear to relieve earache and into the nostrils to relieve sinusitis.

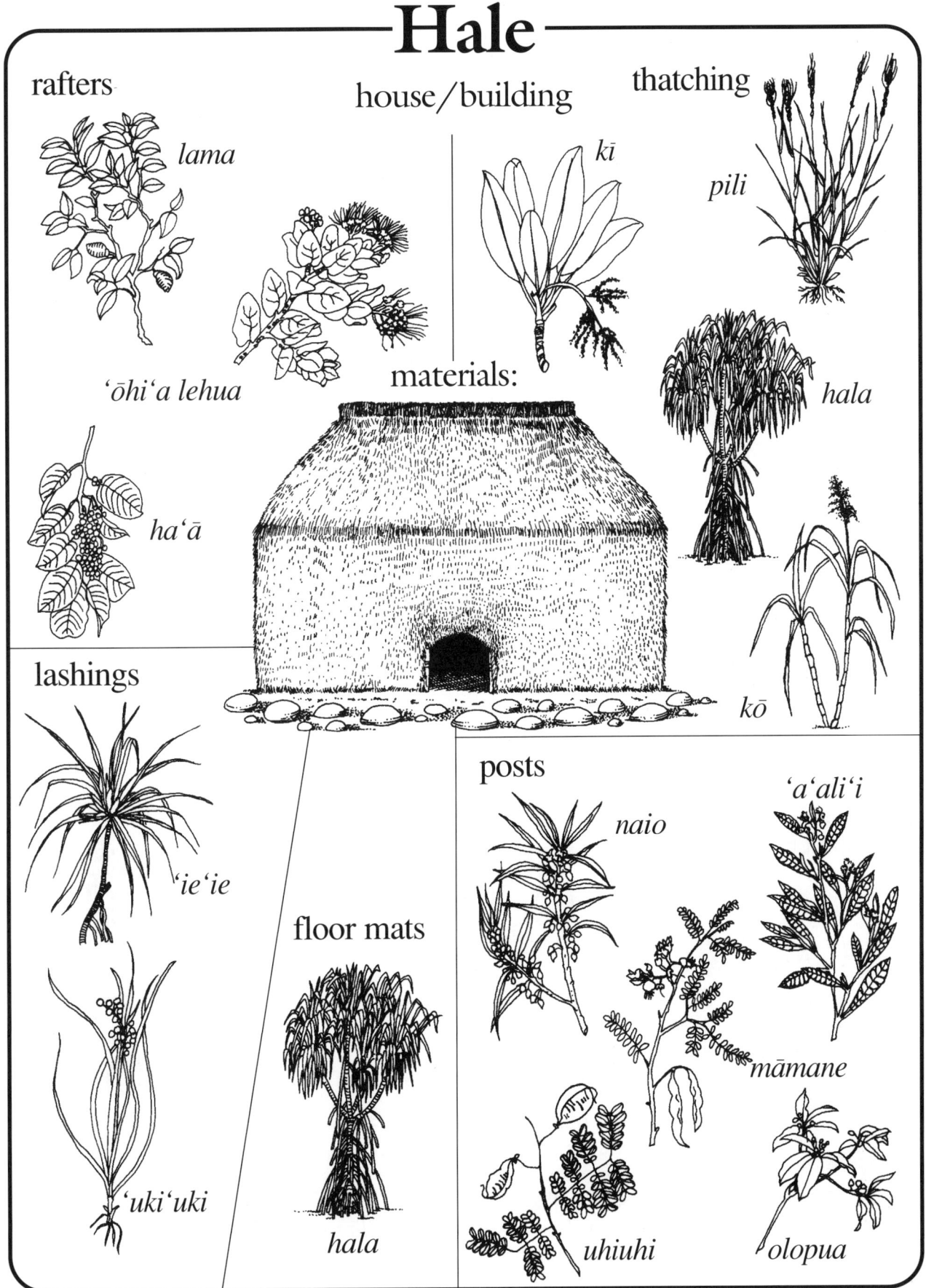

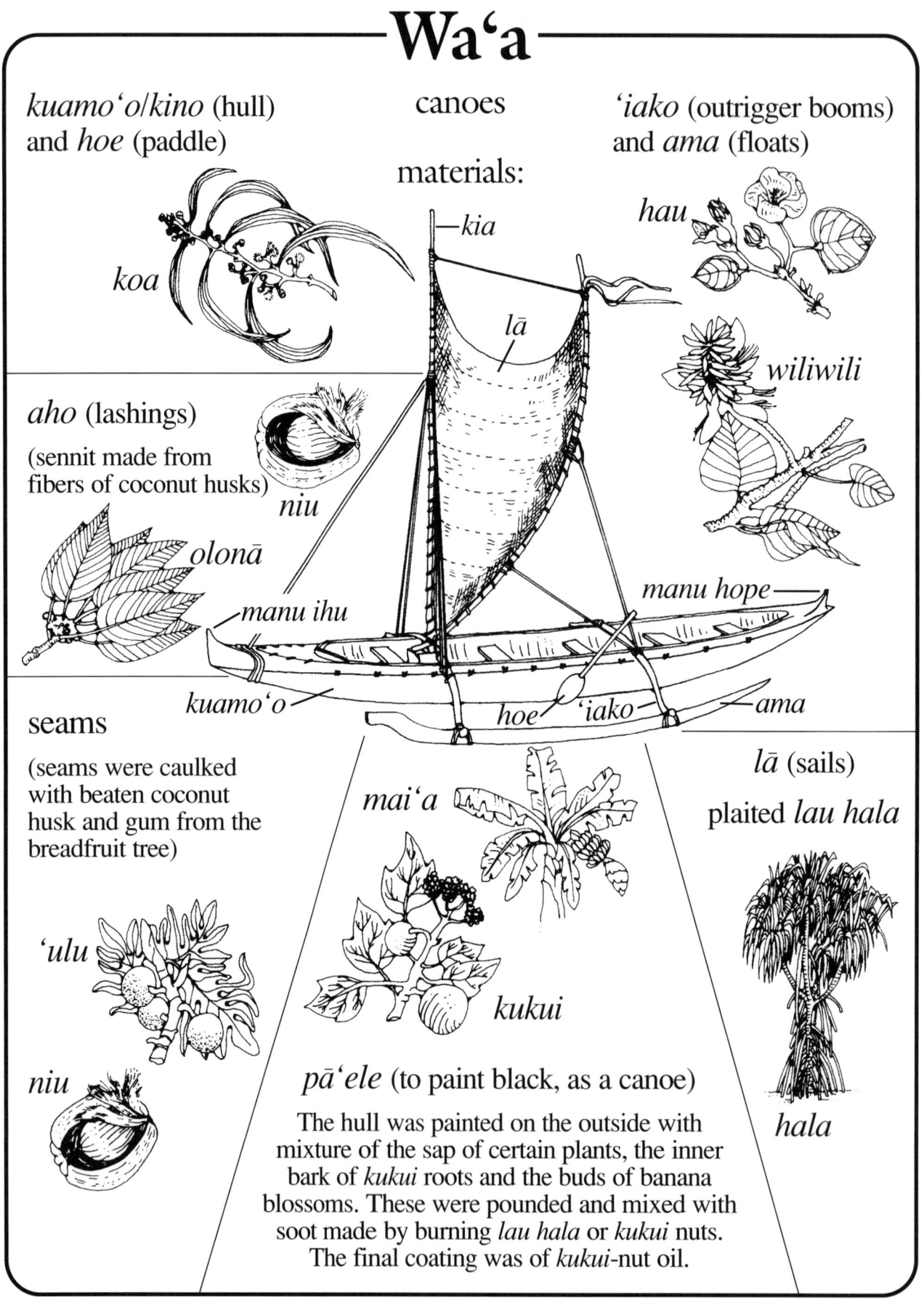

Lāʻau Niu

coconut tree

Uses of the Coconut

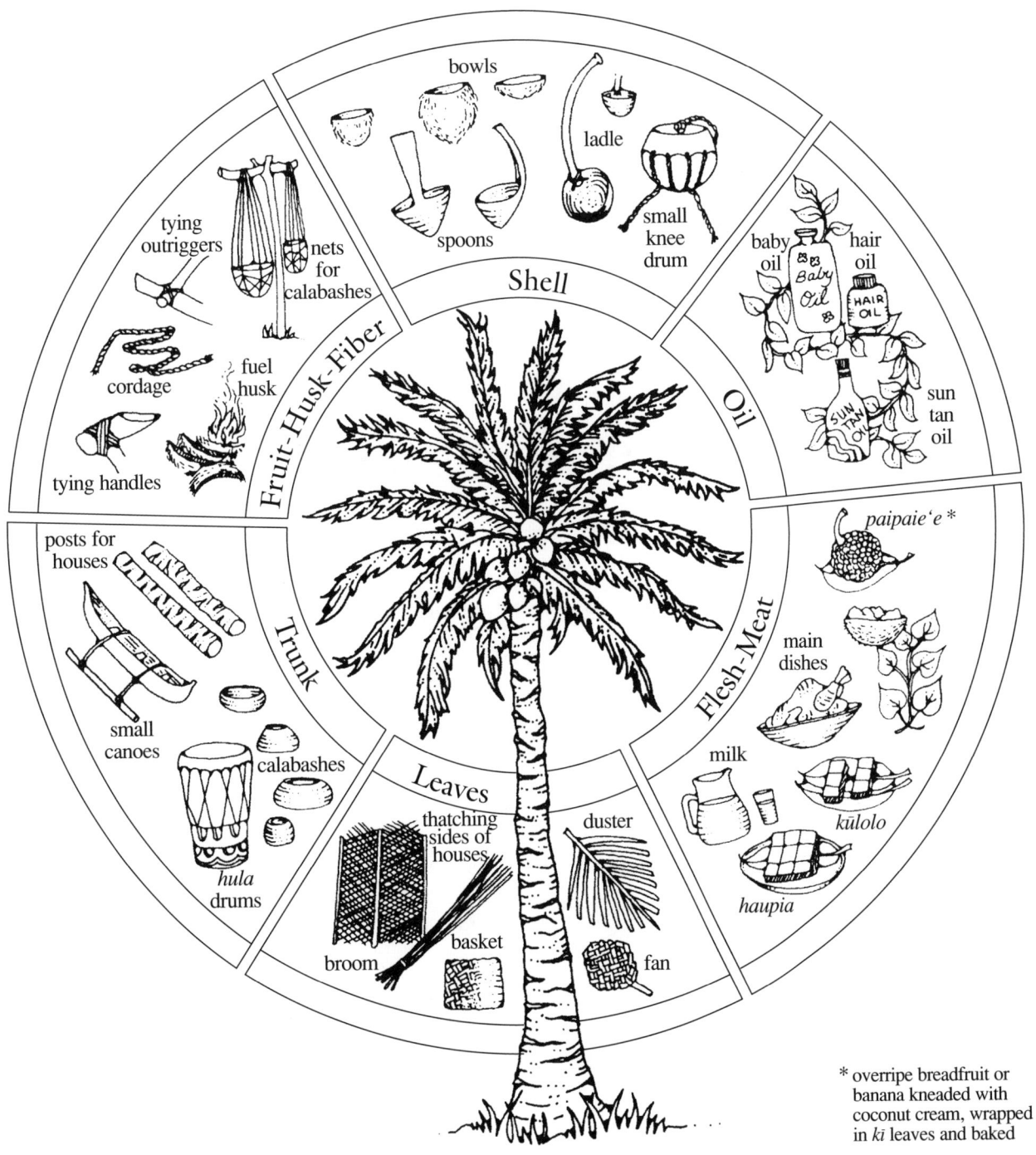

* overripe breadfruit or banana kneaded with coconut cream, wrapped in *kī* leaves and baked

Nā Meakanu Hawai'i

words: Gerri Sasabe
sung to the tune of "Peas, Porridge Hot"

Kalo, mai'a, ulu

Niu, hau olonā

Hala, wauke, kō, kukui

'Uala, 'ōlena

Koa, pia, kī

Nā mea kanu Hawai'i

Waiwai o ka 'āina

E mālama pono!

Mele 'Ōlelo No'eau

words: traditional

Ko kula uka, ko kula kai

Ko kula uka, ko kula kai

'Eā 'eā! 'Eā 'eā! 'Eā 'eā!

Mālama pono i ka 'āina

Mālama pono i ka 'āina

'Eā 'eā! 'Eā 'eā! 'Eā 'eā!

Nā Mea Kanu Word Find

b	a	h	u	p	u	a	ʻ	a	k	o	a	c	e
g	k	ī	f	o	l	o	n	ā	ō	i	n	o	n
p	d	n	i	u	k	l	a	q	r	t	e	b	z
f	l	a	u	y	s	l	p	j	k	a	l	o	b
c	b	n	c	b	a	ʻ	o	p	r	k	ō	j	n
f	n	o	p	h	r	u	l	m	a	i	ʻ	a	k
j	h	u	l	i	z	l	i	w	v	r	b	t	s
p	b	f	r	o	d	u	m	w	a	u	k	e	v
i	g	j	c	s	n	ʻ	a	n	n	g	u	s	h
a	ʻ	s	u	q	m	ā	l	a	m	a	k	p	a
v	ā	p	k	a	i	i	w	n	h	s	u	q	u
d	i	s	a	j	s	n	c	v	u	g	i	k	g
n	n	ʻ	u	a	l	a	b	d	a	r	c	k	t
v	a	r	a	w	z	t	k	a	i	s	u	b	z

ahupuaʻa	hua	kō	mālama	pia
ʻāina	huli	koa	niu	ʻuala
apolima	kai	kukui	noni	uka
hala	kalo	lau	ʻōlena	ʻulu
hau	kī	maiʻa	olonā	wauke
hīnano				

119

"Naughty ʻElepaio"

Word List

aheahe	breeze
hiamoe	fell asleep
hue wai	water gourd
ʻiliʻili	pebble
kanaka	man
kōkua	help
kolohe	naughty
lalo	down
ma uka	towards the upland
manu	bird
nā maka	eyes
nā manamanalima	fingers
poʻo	head
puapua	tail feathers
puka	hole
pūnāwai kuahiwi	mountain spring
wai	water
wāwae	leg

Naughty 'Elepaio

Man was coming down the mountain with a full **water** gourd. Such a long, hot, rough trail all the way **up** to the spring and **down** again! In the shade of a rock he stopped to rest. A little **breeze** reached him with cooling **fingers**. **Man** sat **down**, leaned against the cool rock and **fell asleep**.

Along came a small, curious *'elepaio* **bird**. He lighted on a tree to look at **man**. Then he flew to the rock and cocked his **head** this way and that as he made sure **man** was asleep. At last he hopped down to the **water gourd** and examined it with his bright **eyes**. Back went his **head** and hammer, hammer, hammer, his small bill struck the **gourd** until a tiny **hole** appeared. *'Elepaio* watched the **water** trickle through the **hole** then flew back to the tree.

Man awoke and picked up his **gourd**. How light it felt! Then he noticed a wet spot where the **gourd** had rested. He saw the **hole**. "Who has done this?" he asked angrily. He caught sight of *'elepaio*. "Naughty bird!" he shouted and aimed a **pebble**.

The **pebble** struck the leg of *'elepaio* and away flew the angry **bird**. He found *'io*, the hawk. "O friend *'io*," he shouted, "help me! Help me to punish **man**!"

"What has **man** done?" asked *'io* sharply. "If **man** has harmed a little bird, he shall indeed be punished!"

"He threw a stone and hit my **leg**. See!" and *'elepaio* limped as he hopped along a twig.

"Why did **man** do that?" *'io* asked. "What had you done?"

"Nothing at all!" answered *'elepaio* innocently. "I only pecked a little **hole** in his **water gourd**."

"And let out all the **water** that he brought from the **mountain spring**!" *'io* exclaimed. "I don't blame **man** for being angry! Be off, you naughty bird!"

'Elepaio went to *pueo*, the owl. "I need your **help**, *pueo*," he said. "I need your help to punish **man**. See what he has done to me!"

"Poor little **bird**!" said *pueo* kindly. "What a cruel thing for **man** to do." "What had you done to him?"

"I didn't even touch him!" *'elepaio* exclaimed. "I only pecked a **hole** in his **water gourd**, a tiny hole."

"Oh naughty *'elepaio*! All the water could run out a tiny **hole**. I don't blame **man** for being angry. Be off with you!"

So *'elepaio* flew away and found *'i'iwi*, but *'i'iwi* too called him a **naughty** bird. At last he came to *'amakihi* flitting about among *lehua* blossoms. "O, *'amakihi*," he cried, "see what **man** has done! See how lame I am all because of that cruel **man**!"

'Amakihi hopped about watching the limping **bird**. "Too bad! Too bad!" he chirped. "What had you done, *'elepaio*? What had you done?"

"Nothing! Nothing but peck a tiny **hole** in his **water gourd**!"

"Served you right!" chirped *'amakihi*, hopping about and shaking his tail as if he laughed at *'elepaio*. "Served you right!"

"Useless bird!" shouted *'elepaio* angrily.

"Maybe I'm useless," chirped *'amakihi*, shaking his tail again, "but at least I don't go about making trouble."

Told by Mary Kawena Pūku'i

Nā Kumu Waiwai O Ke Kai

Ocean Studies

Fishing was the most varied and extensive food gathering work of the Hawaiians. They developed expert skills in catching fish and had expert knowledge of the ocean. The area of fishing usually extended from the seashore out towards the horizon. They used special methods and equipment in catching different fish and practiced conservation by declaring certain fish *kapu* (forbidden or sacred) during certain times of the year.

The skilled fisherman had knowledge of the stars, of the winds, of the currents and of the clouds. He had knowledge of, and respect for, the traditions and customs of fishing. This vast knowledge was passed down orally from the informed and experienced *kūpuna* (elders) to the interested youths.

Fishermen relied on their knowledge, skills and experience to help them catch fish, the main protein in their diet, and other foods from the sea. They shared these foods with their *'ohana* (extended family) and other members of the community.

Ke Kai

Julie Williams

O SEAS that touch Hawaiʻi's shore,
    "Pulled" by the moon from Ocean's floor;
        Rising high—in the tide flows,
        Falling low—out the tide goes.
            Pae ke kai!

O WINDS that blow—gentle or strong,
    Create the waves that surge along;
        The waves that break all day, all night,
        The waves with crests, like caps of white.
            Pā ka makani!

O CURRENTS, deep and flowing forth,
    Made by winds: east, west, south, north:
        The winds that often change their course,
        The sea grows rough against their force.
            Ke kai koʻo!

O FISHERMAN, behold the sea!
    Alive with fish and creatures, free;
        Know when to go and what to do,
        And where to go in your canoe.
            ʻIke ka lawaiʻa!

O NAVIGATOR, watch ahead!
    By nature's signs you can be led;
        By winds and waves and birds that fly,
        By clouds and stars and moon on high.
            Makaʻala ka hoʻokele!

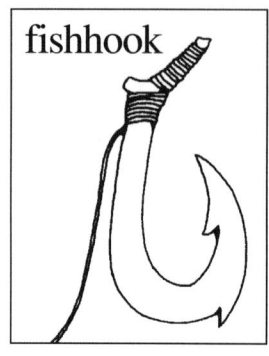

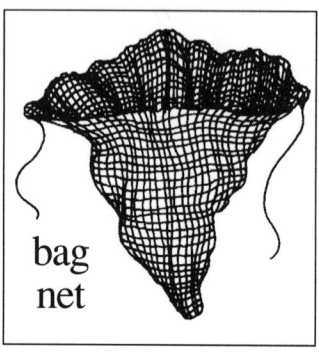

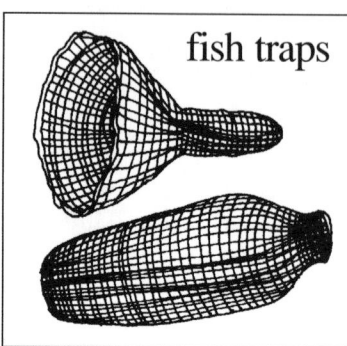

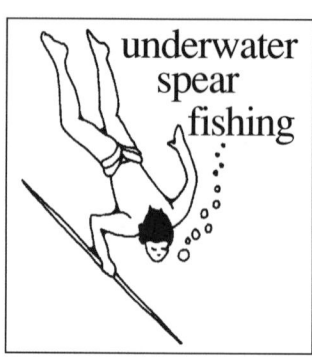

fishhook

bag
net

fish traps

underwater
spear
fishing

Nā I'a A Me Nā 'Ano Lawai'a

Fishes and Fishing Methods

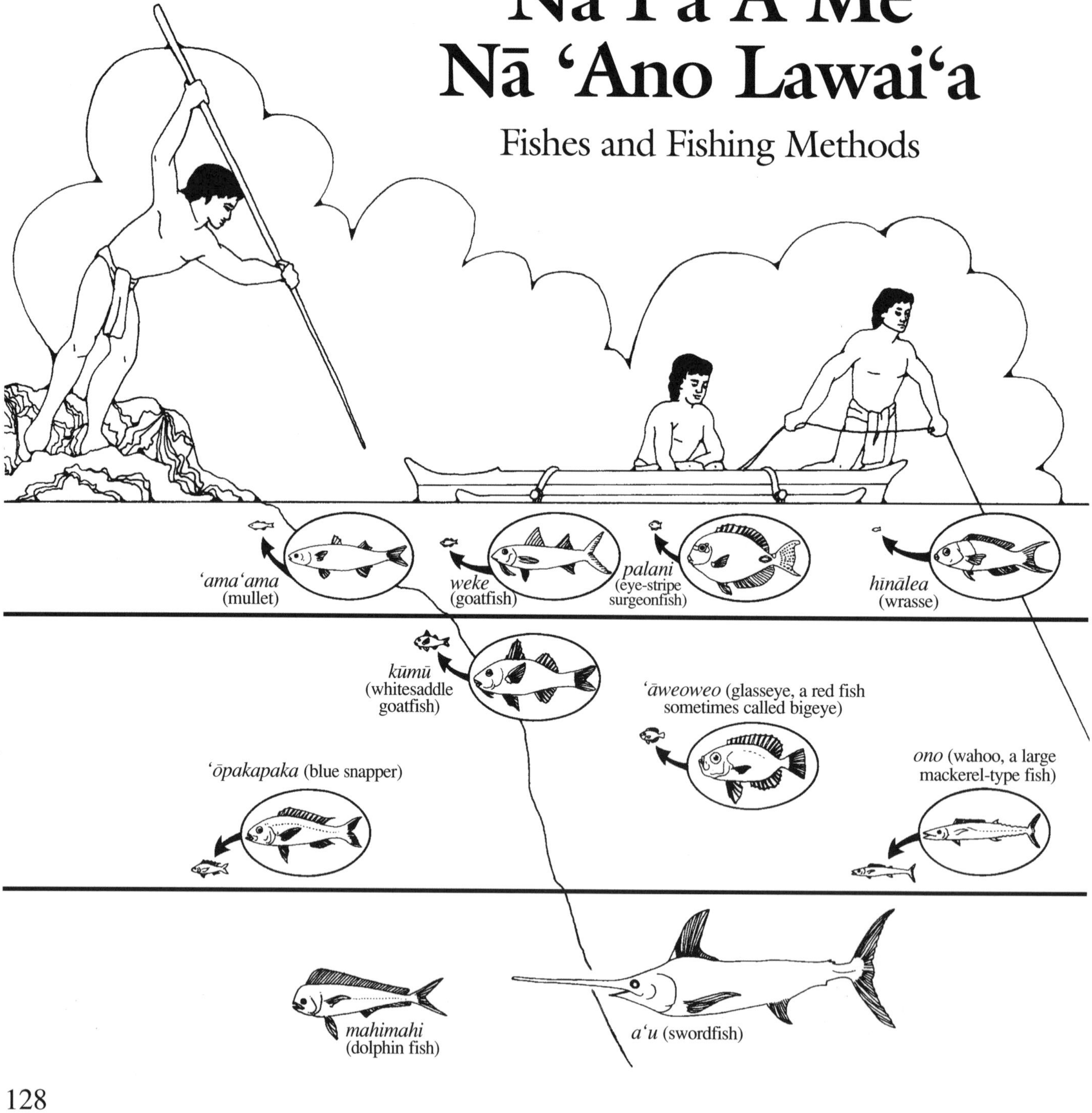

'ama'ama (mullet)
weke (goatfish)
palani (eye-stripe surgeonfish)
hīnālea (wrasse)
kūmū (whitesaddle goatfish)
'āweoweo (glasseye, a red fish sometimes called bigeye)
'ōpakapaka (blue snapper)
ono (wahoo, a large mackerel-type fish)
mahimahi (dolphin fish)
a'u (swordfish)

torch fishing
scoop net
dip net
he'e (octopus) lure

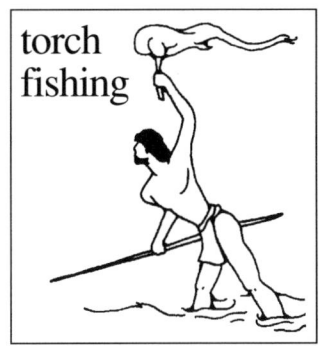

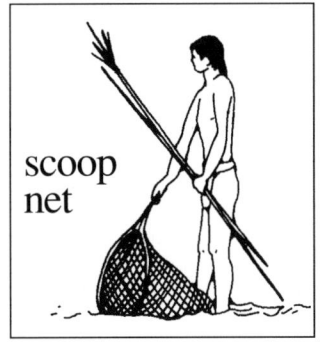

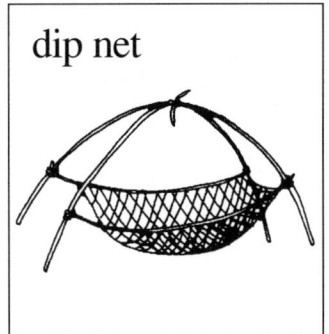

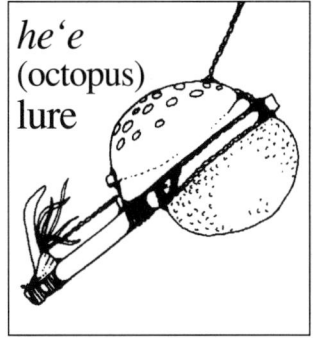

Fish and *poi* (cooked taro corms, rarely breadfruit, pounded and thinned with water) were the main foods of the early Hawaiians. The Hawaiian fishermen knew the seas, the waves, the currents, the tides and the habits of different fish. He knew where to go for different kinds of fish, when to go and what to use to catch a certain kind of fish.

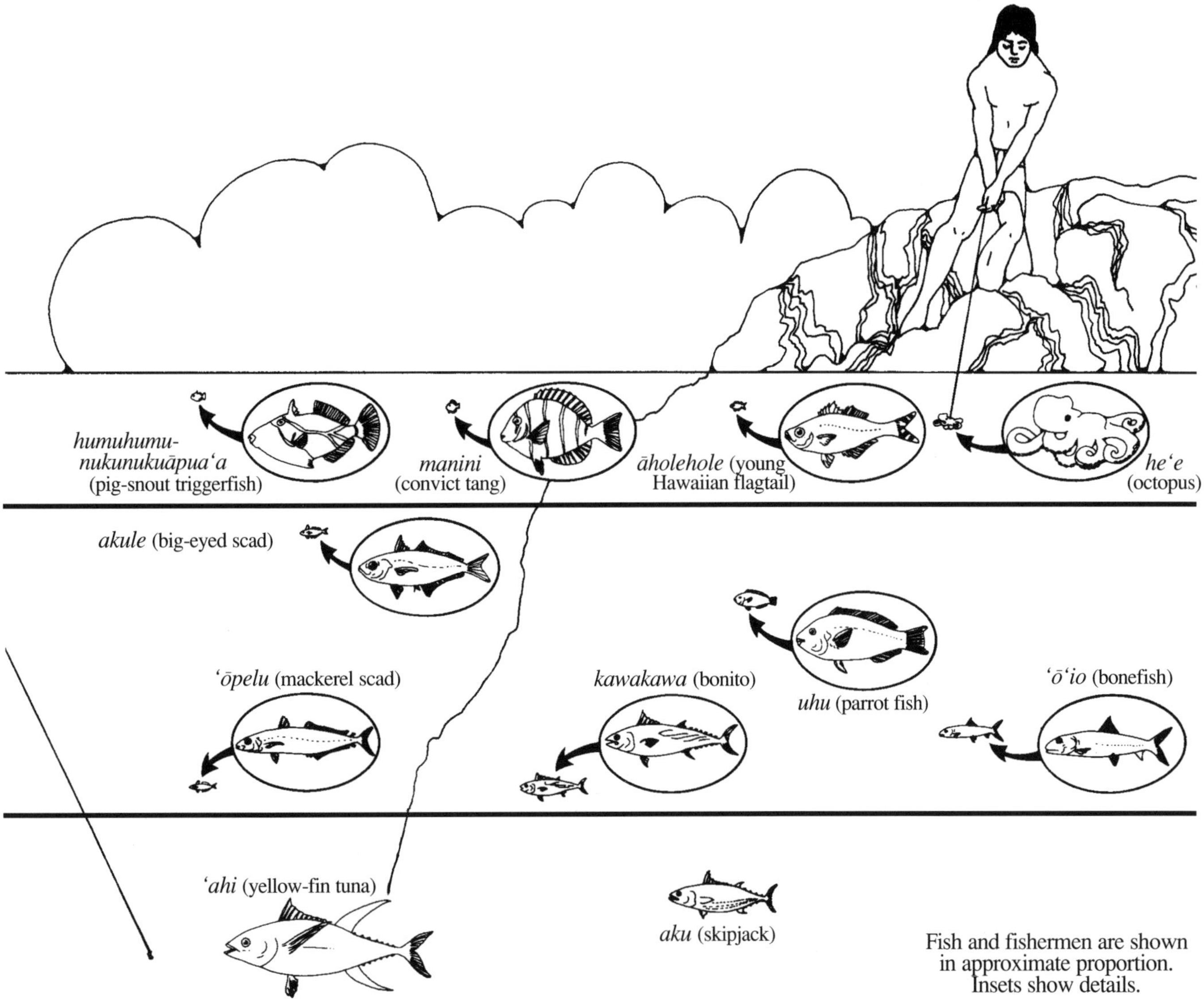

humuhumu-nukunukuāpua'a (pig-snout triggerfish)
manini (convict tang)
āholehole (young Hawaiian flagtail)
he'e (octopus)
akule (big-eyed scad)
uhu (parrot fish)
'ōpelu (mackerel scad)
kawakawa (bonito)
'ō'io (bonefish)
'ahi (yellow-fin tuna)
aku (skipjack)
Fish and fishermen are shown in approximate proportion. Insets show details.

'ama'ama — 8"

weke

āholehole

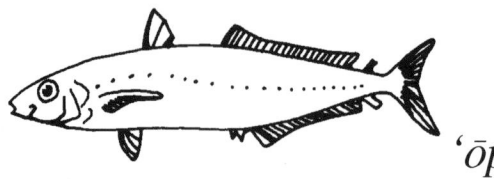
'ōpelu

akule

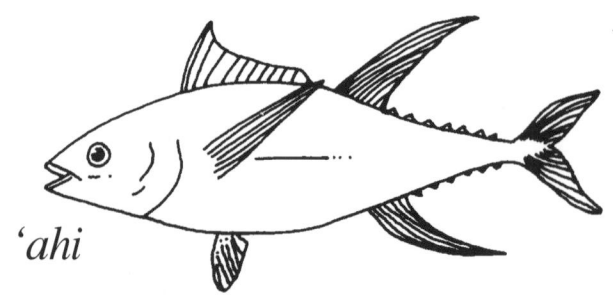
'ahi

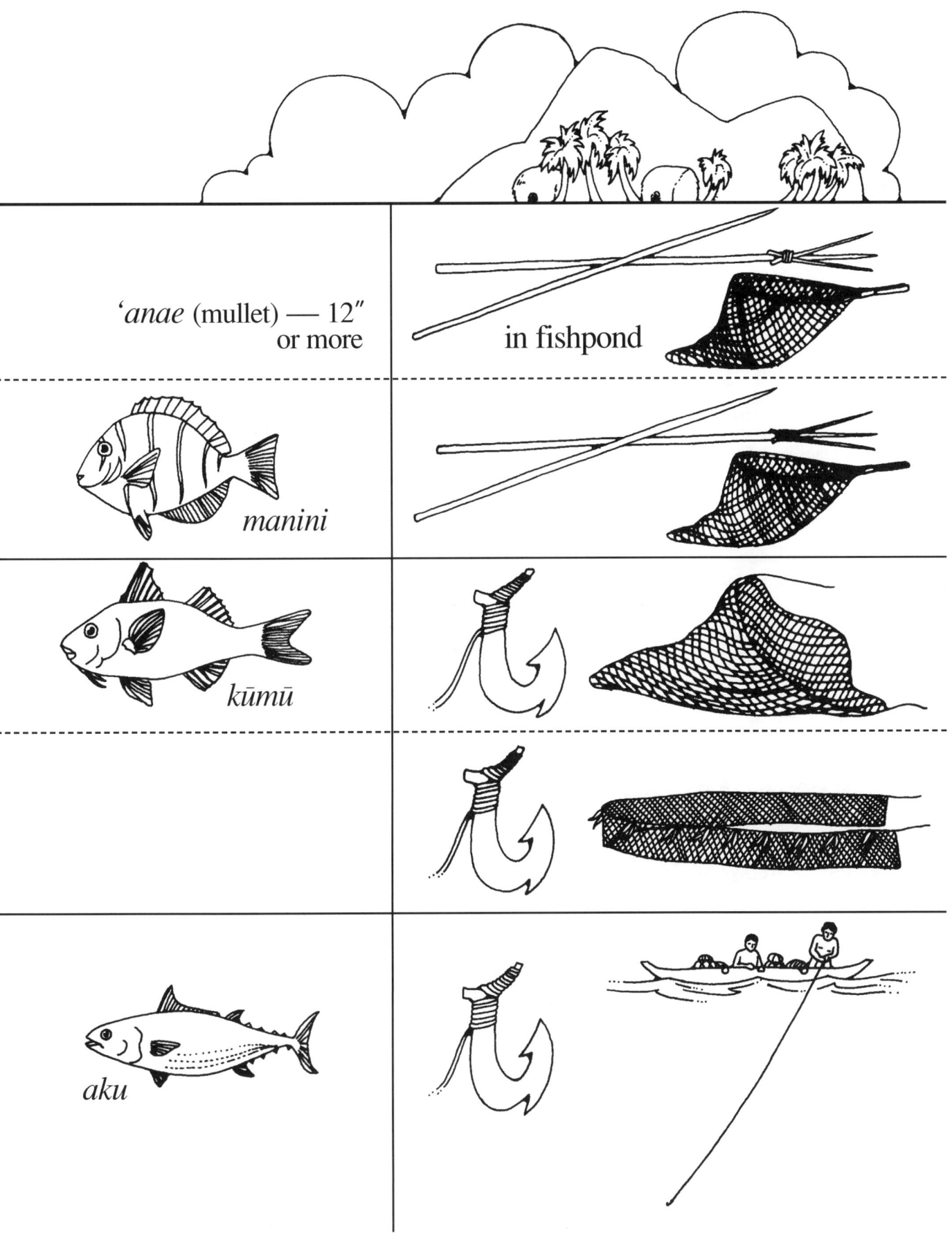

Loko i'a
fishpond

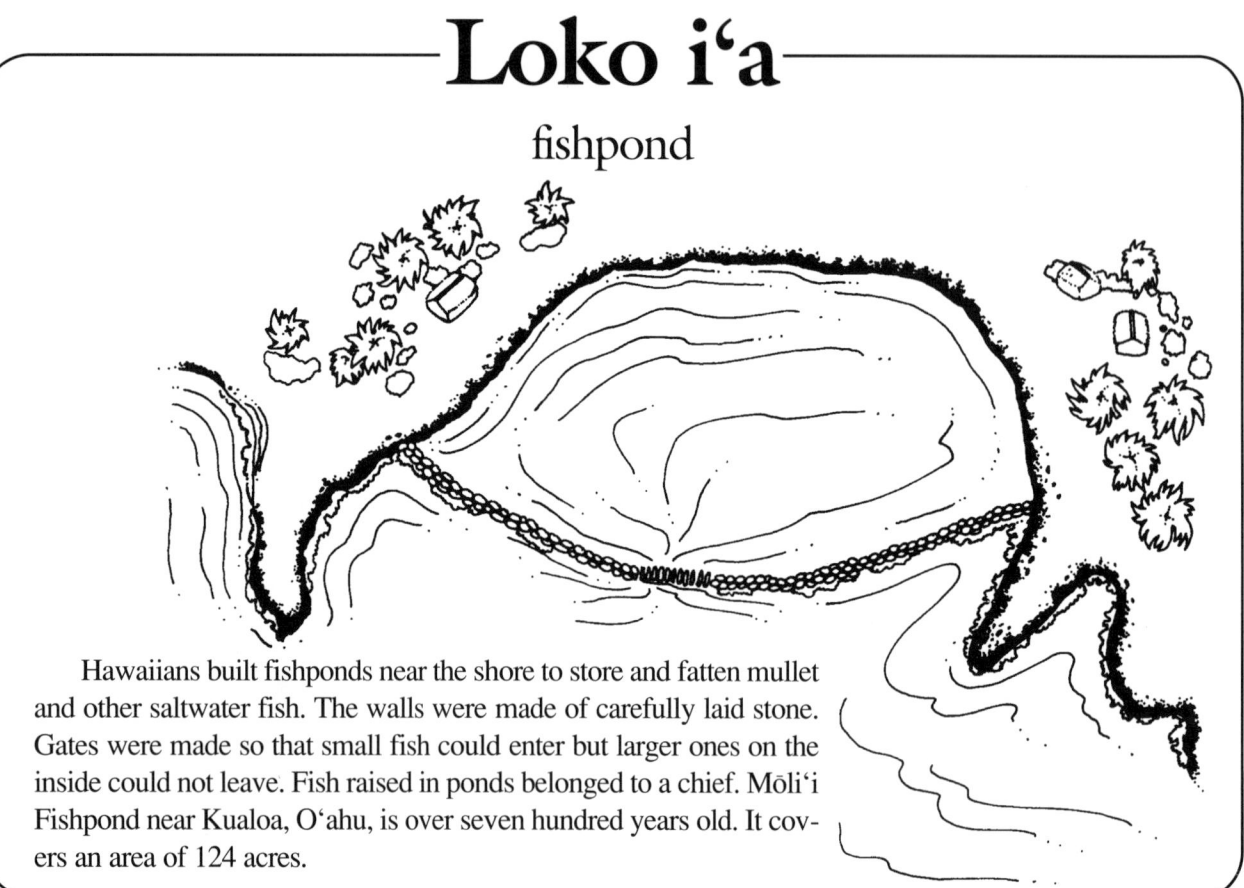

Hawaiians built fishponds near the shore to store and fatten mullet and other saltwater fish. The walls were made of carefully laid stone. Gates were made so that small fish could enter but larger ones on the inside could not leave. Fish raised in ponds belonged to a chief. Mōli'i Fishpond near Kualoa, O'ahu, is over seven hundred years old. It covers an area of 124 acres.

Hukilau

Sometimes a whole village took part in a type of fishing called *hukilau* (net fishing). *Huki* means pull and *lau* means leaf. Long ropes were hung with leaves, usually *lā'ī* (*kī*, or ti, leaves). The leaves would frighten the fish into a larger net. Then the net was pulled ashore. The hundreds of fish were divided among all those who helped.

Limu

seaweed

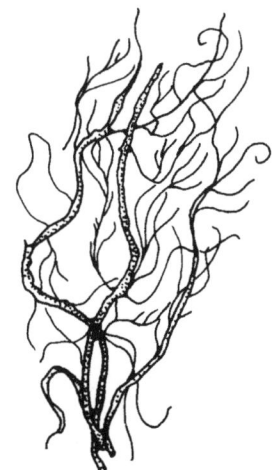

limu ʻeleʻele
(long green *limu*)

limu kohu
(soft, tufted and red *limu*)

limu līpoa
(much branched and brown *limu*)

Food

Limu was salted and eaten raw primarily as a relish with meat and fish.

Medicine

Limu was used on bruises and as a poultice for boils.

Sea Animals

Pipipi are small sea snails found on rocks. They are cooked in sea water and the meat pried out and eaten. Shells were pierced and strung for *lei* (garlands and wreaths).

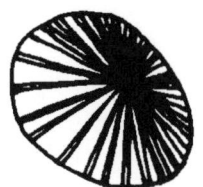

ʻOpihi are limpets. The favorite kind has yellow meat and clings to rocks where the waves were the roughest. The meat is salted and eaten raw. The sharp-edged shells were used for scooping, peeling and scraping.

Wana are sea urchins with sharp spines. The meat and fluid are salted and eaten. They are considered the most delicious of the urchins.

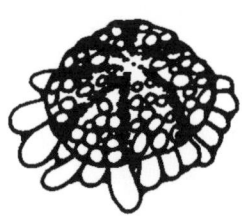

Hāʻukeʻuke are sea urchins with short or flattened spines. They have more fluid than meat and are not considered as tasty as *wana*.

Nā Mahina
the moons

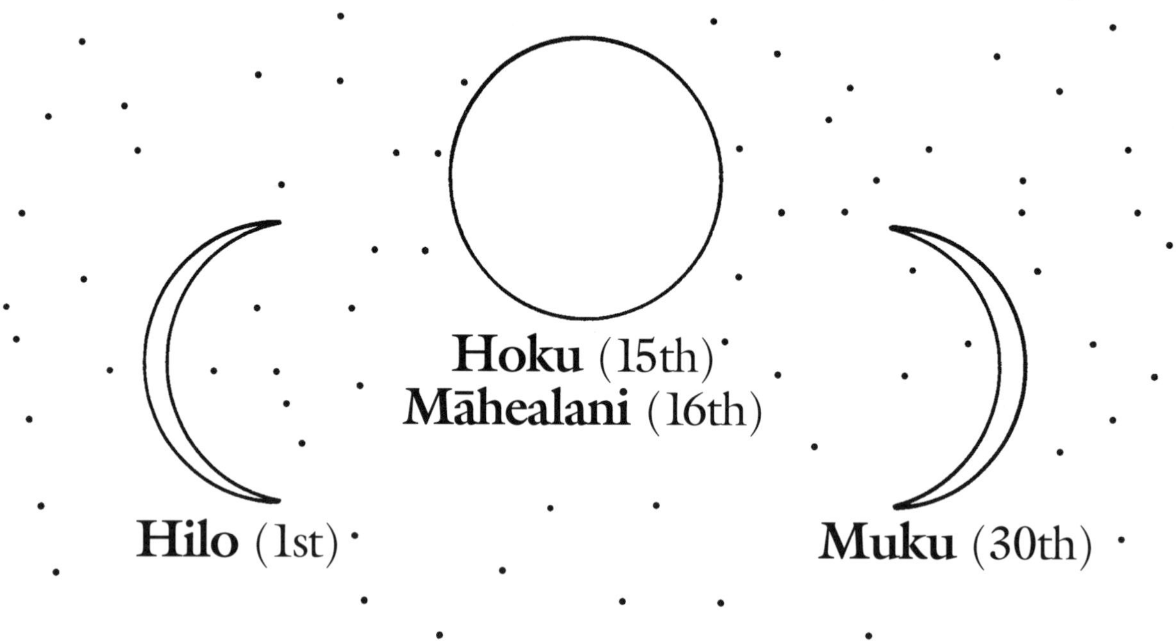

Hoku (15th)
Māhealani (16th)

Hilo (1st)

Muku (30th)

Nā Hōkū
the stars

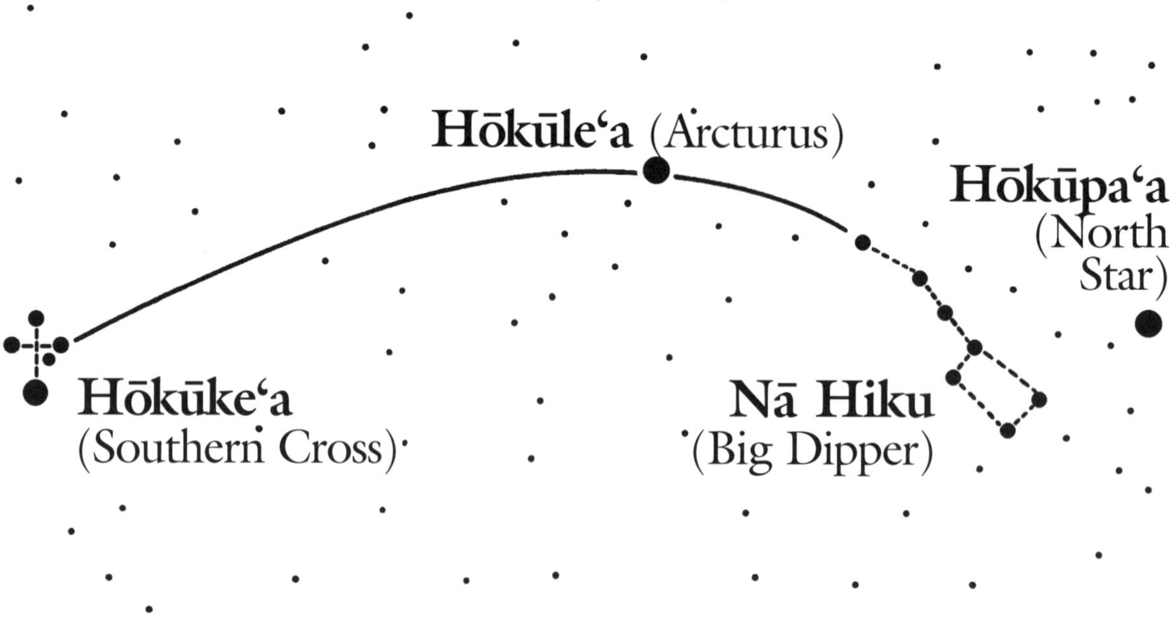

Hōkūle'a (Arcturus)

Hōkūpa'a (North Star)

Hōkūke'a (Southern Cross)

Nā Hiku (Big Dipper)

Nā Makani
the winds

northeast tradewinds **Moaʻe**

Hanauma Bay

southerly or leeward wind **Kona**

Visiting Hanauma Bay

Hoe Wa'a
the canoe paddler

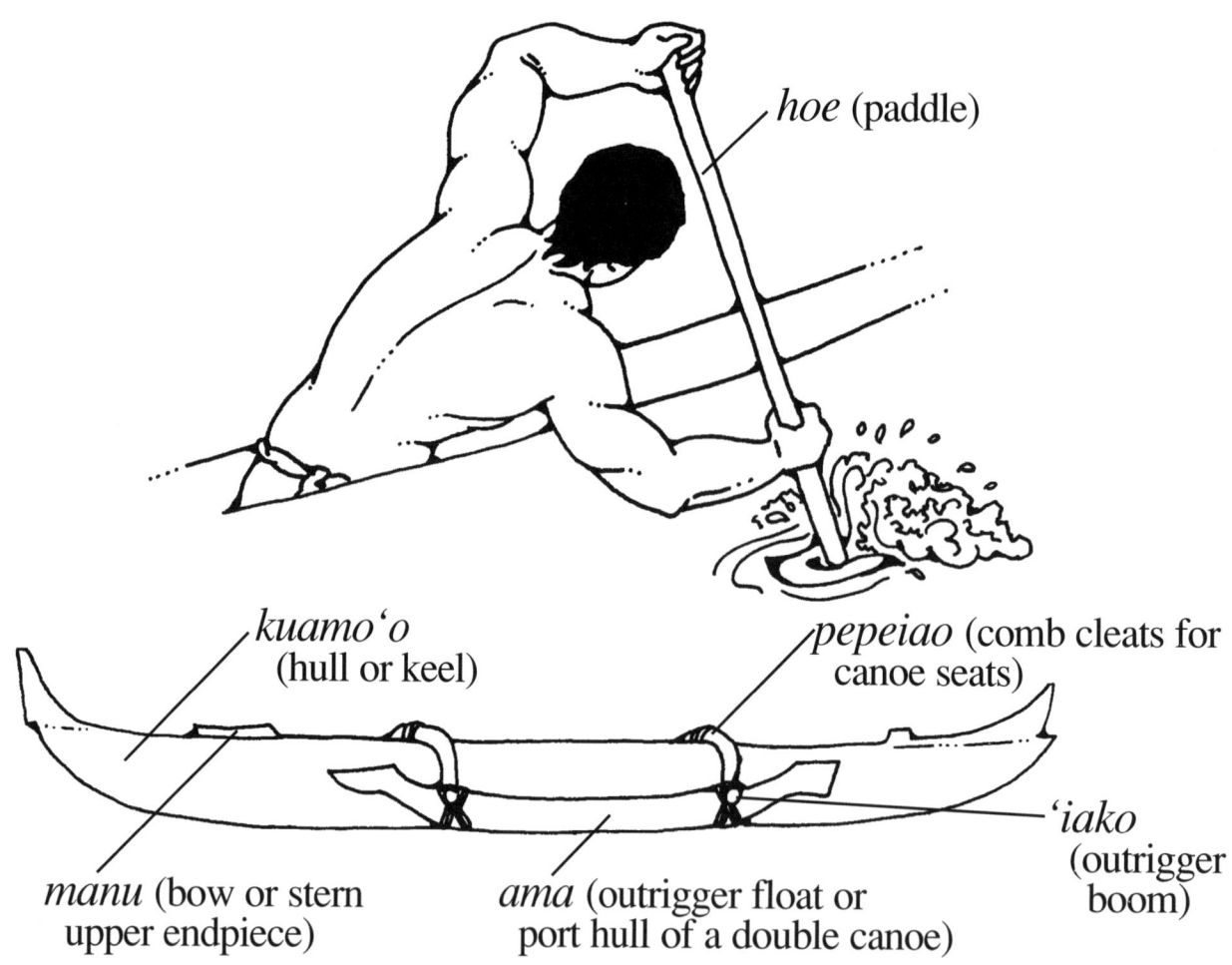

hoe (paddle)

kuamo'o (hull or keel)

pepeiao (comb cleats for canoe seats)

'iako (outrigger boom)

manu (bow or stern upper endpiece)

ama (outrigger float or port hull of a double canoe)

Hoe Aku!
Paddle Ahead!

words and music: unknown

Hoe aku i kou wa'a	Paddle your canoe
Hoe, hoe!	Paddle, paddle!
Nānā i ka Hōkūpa'a	Look at the north star
Hahai i ka Hōkūle'a	Follow Hōkūle'a
Auē! 'O Hawai'i kēia!	Oh! This is Hawai'i!

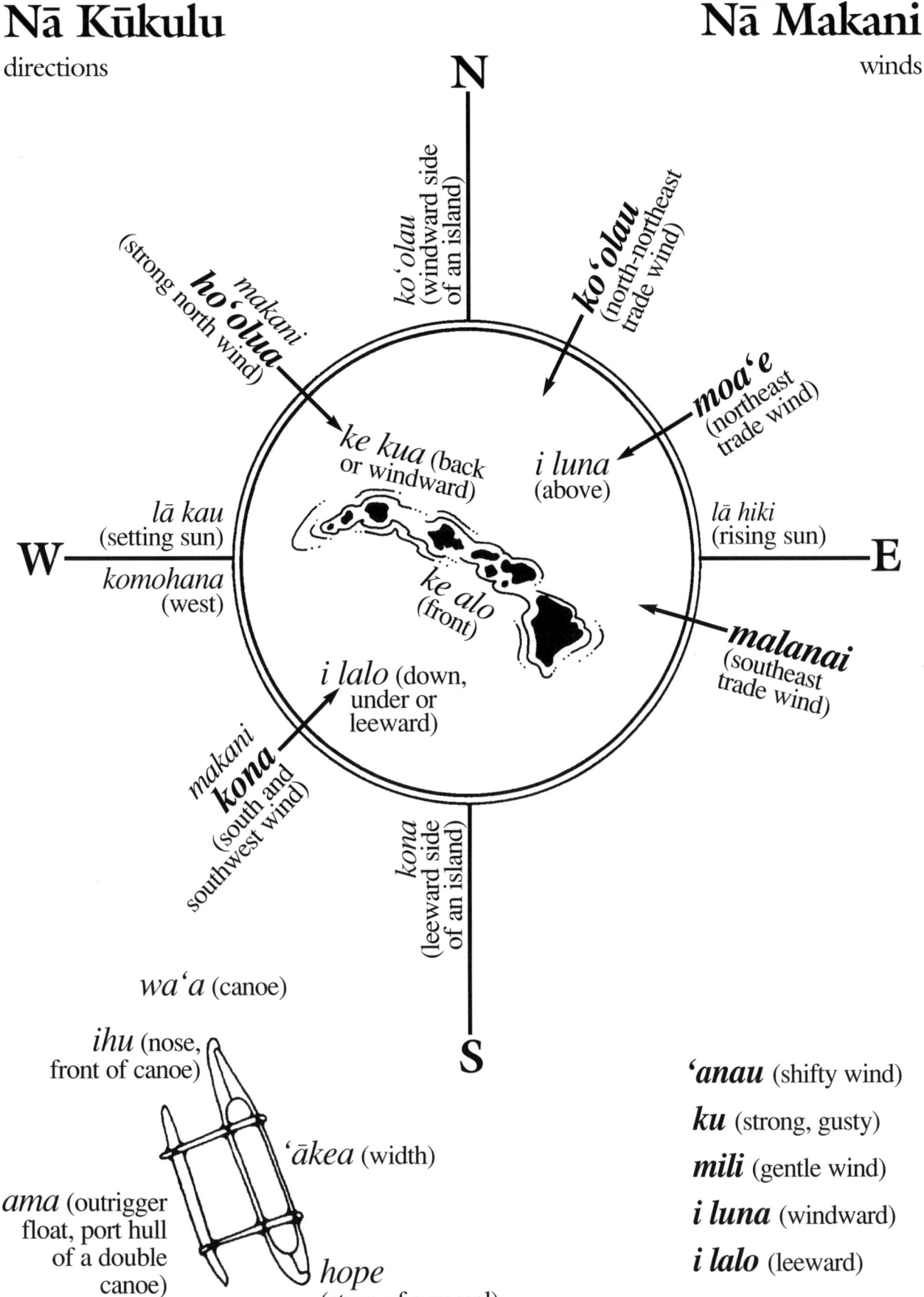

"Māui's Fishing"

Word List

aho	line
'au	swim
hoe	paddled
ho'omana'o	remember
hope	stern of a vessel
huki	pull
huki a'e	pulling up
i'a	fish
iwi	bone
kahakai	beaches
kai	sea water
ko'a	offshore fishing ground
lawai'a	fishing
makau	fishhook
manō	shark
mea 'ai	food
moana	ocean
nalu	surf
pōhaku	rocks
wa'a	canoe

Māui's Fishing

Māui-of-a-thousand-tricks was a name given the hero by people who admired him. But his brothers, who went **fishing** with him, did not like his tricks. "When Māui is with us we do the work and he pulls in the fish." That was what the brothers said to each other and they left Māui at home.

One day Māui made a **fishhook**. It was carved from **bone** and as he shaped it Māui prayed. He prayed to the gods to make this a **hook** of mighty power.

Next morning he asked his brothers to let him go **fishing** with them. "No," they answered as they launched their **canoe**. Māui scrambled onto the **stern** but the brothers pushed him off. "**Swim** ashore, tricky one," they said and **paddled** away.

That night when they returned Māui met them. "Did you catch many **fish**?" he asked.

"The **sea** is empty," they answered. "We caught nothing but a **shark** and it is a kind not good for **food**."

"You should have taken me," said Māui.

"You could catch **fish** where there are no **fish**?" his brothers asked, laughing at him.

"Take me tomorrow and you shall see," Māui told them.

The next day they let him enter the **canoe**. The brothers **fished** but caught nothing. As for Māui, he tied the **hook** of power to his **line** but did not cast it into the **ocean**. "Why don't you **fish**?" the brothers asked. "You boasted that you could pull something from this empty **sea**. Why don't you do it?"

"Not here!" Māui replied. "**Paddle** farther out."

The brothers did. At last they said, "This is our **off-shore fishing ground**. Now let us see you **fish**."

"**Paddle** farther," Māui repeated.

"But this is far enough. This is our **off-shore fishing ground**, we tell you."

"If I am to catch **fish** you must **paddle** farther," Māui answered. The brothers did. They **paddled** so far from their island that they could no longer see the line of **surf** breaking on **rocks** and **beaches**.

"This is far enough," Māui said at last. "Now listen to my words. Turn the **canoe** and **paddle** back toward home. You will know when I have caught a **fish**, for you will

feel its pull. Then dig your **paddles** into the **sea** with all your strength. **Paddle** toward home and don't look back. **Remember**, don't turn to look back!"

The brothers headed the **canoe** toward home and **paddled**. They knew when Māui caught a **fish**. They knew by its mighty pull that seemed to be carrying them away from land. They dug their **paddles** into the **water** with all their strength.

Māui was playing his **fish**. As he struggled he panted to his brothers, "**Paddle, Paddle!** Don't look back!"

"What kind of a **fish** has Māui caught?" the brothers wondered. "What can it be that pulls so mightily?"

Filled with wonder, one turned to look. "Brothers!" he shouted. "It is the land Māui has caught. He is **pulling up** islands!"

Everyone stopped **paddling** and turned to stare.

"See what you have done!" cried Māui angrily. "I was going to **pull** up a great land, but because you stopped **paddling** I have only these islands!"

And that, so the story says, is the way our Hawaiian Islands came above the **ocean**.

Adapted from
Legends of Ma-ui—A Demi God of Polynesia and of His Mother Hina
by W.D. Westervelt,
The Hawaiian Gazette Co., Ltd. (1910)

Nā Huaka'i Māka'ika'i
Field Trips

To enhance the morning studies of Hawaiian culture, afternoon field trips are planned to various places on Oʻahu such as Sea Life Park, Maunaʻala (the site of the Royal Mausoleum), ʻIolani Palace, Bernice Pauahi Bishop Museum Planetarium and the Polynesian Cultural Center. On the Kamehameha Schools campus visits are made to Bishop Memorial Chapel and the Heritage Center.

Visits to these sites add to your experience of Hawaiian culture and further a deeper understanding of Hawaiʻi and the rich heritage of the Hawaiian people.

1
Ka Huakaʻi ʻEkahi

Sea Life Park—Makapuʻu

Sea Life Park, located at Makapuʻu in the Kona district of Oʻahu, is the field trip site for the Ocean Studies class. Visiting the Hawaiian Reef Tank you will learn about sea life dwelling in various ocean zones—caves, rock and coral sheltering areas, bottom, mid-water and surface. In the Hawaiʻi Ocean Theater and at Whaler's Cove you will learn more about the Pacific bottlenose dolphin as well as other sea mammals.

2
Ka Huaka'i 'Elua

Mauna'ala—The Royal Mausoleum in Nu'uanu Valley (A)
and
The He'eia State Park Glass-Bottom Boat Excursion (B)

A.

In old Hawai'i the bones of some chiefs were placed in a special house in a *heiau* (place of worship). The bones of other chiefs were hidden in caves. When Kamehameha I died in 1819 his bones were hidden by Hoapili and Ho'olulu. They were his trusted friends. They kept their secret well. The bones have never been found.

In 1824 Kamehameha II and Queen Kamāmalu died in London of the measles. Their bodies were returned to Honolulu in beautiful wood caskets. Since that time the bodies of the royal dead have not been buried in caves. Instead they have been placed in caskets made from Hawaiian woods.

At first these caskets were kept in a small stone mausoleum on the grounds of 'Iolani Palace. A mausoleum is a large tomb or grave. Later, these caskets were moved to Mauna'ala, the site of a larger mausoleum built in 1865 in Nu'uanu Valley. Mauna'ala means "fragrant mountain."

The mausoleum is a stone building designed like a chapel. It was fitted with sturdy racks around its inside walls to support the caskets. But this plan did not work very well. So three crypts were built for the caskets of the royal dead. A crypt is an underground room or vault used as a burial place.

147

The Kamehameha crypt is marked by a red-brown granite stone. Printed on the stone are the names of those buried in the crypt. The name of Bernice Pauahi is on the side that faces Nuʻuanu Stream. Charles Reed Bishop died in 1915. His ashes were placed on the casket of his wife, Bernice Pauahi. Then the crypt was sealed.

Steep stairs go down into the Kalākaua crypt. On the central wall are two marble slabs. Printed in gold are the names of King Kalākaua and Queen Kapiʻolani. The names on the right wall belong to members of the Kalākaua family. In the center is Hawaiʻi's last ruler, Queen Liliʻuokalani. Most of the names on the left wall belong to members of Kapiʻolani's family. Prince Jonah Kūhiō Kalanianaʻole is on the left side.

The third crypt is the Wyllie tomb. It contains the bodies of people close to Queen Emma, wife of Kamehameha IV. There is also a tombstone honoring Mr. Bishop.

The stone building that first held the caskets was made into a chapel. The walls are covered with *koa* (the largest native forest tree, *Acacia koa*) wood. The altar pieces are also made of *koa*. Special services are held here.

The custodian lives on the grounds. It is a tradition that the custodian be a descendant of Hoʻolulu.

In the words of Kuhina Nui Healani Doane, as spoken on November 23, 1987, at the Rededication of the Royal Mausoleum Chapel: "Because of [Queen Emma's] efforts the *aliʻi* rest at peace here at Maunaʻala on the only parcel of land in the Hawaiian islands placed outside the public domain. In respect for the dignity and ancestral authority of the *aliʻi* only the Hawaiian flag flies over Maunaʻala."

B.

This *huakaʻi* (field trip) takes you on a glass-bottom boat onto the ocean off Kāneʻohe town along the windward coastline of Oʻahu. As you enjoy the thrilling ride keep in mind that you are traveling on part of the same ocean highway which served as the principal means of transportation for early Hawaiians.

Whether traveling a short distance from one village to another, longer trips from island to island or still longer voyages from one island group to another, Hawaiians were always at home on the sea. They were experts in constructing strong and efficient canoes. Ancient Hawaiians skillfully navigated over vast ocean expanses using their keen knowledge of the sun, moon and stars and generations of experience in understanding the winds and clouds, ocean currents and swells, changes in the colors of sea and sky and the habits of birds.

3
Ka Huaka'i 'Ekolu

Bernice Pauahi Bishop Memorial Chapel and Heritage Center (A)
and
'Iolani Palace (B)

A.

The Princess Bernice Pauahi Bishop Memorial Chapel and Heritage Center were dedicated in 1988. The chapel is the home of the Bishop Memorial Church. It serves the school community by conducting weekly Sunday services, devotional services and classes throughout the school year.

The Heritage Center houses many of Princess Pauahi's personal belongings.

B.

'Iolani Palace was once the home of King Kalākaua and Queen Lili'uokalani. Construction began on December 31, 1879. The new palace was completed and furnished by 1882 at a cost of $360,000. It was the site of many grand events including King Kalākaua's coronation in 1883. In 1893 'Iolani Palace was the site of the overthrow of the monarchy. Queen Lili'uokalani was imprisoned there in 1895 following a counter-revolution attempt to restore her to the throne.

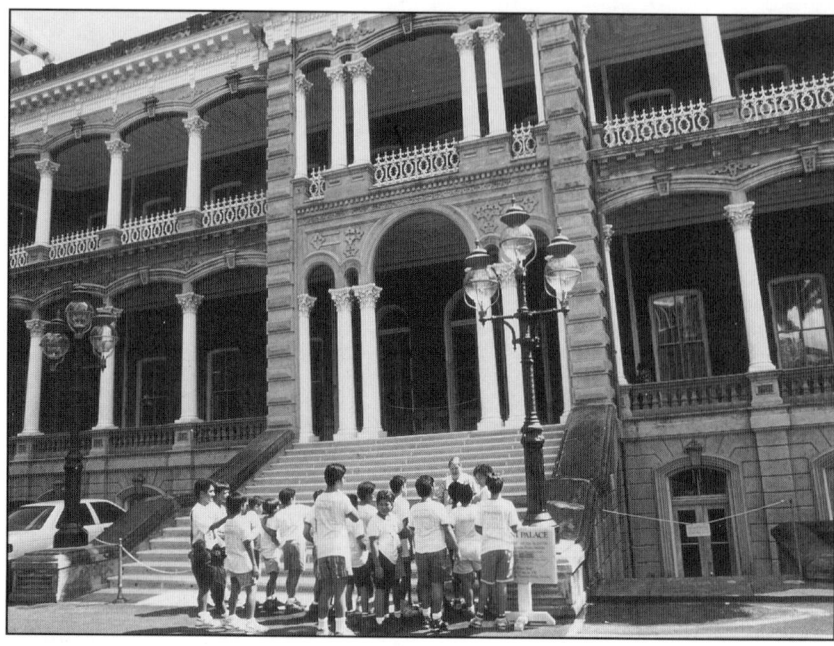

'Iolani Palace served as the official capitol building of Hawai'i until 1968 when the new state capitol building was completed. Since that time the legislature has appropriated about six million dollars to restore 'Iolani Palace. It is the only royal palace in the United States.

The statue of Queen Lili'uokalani stands on the mall between 'Iolani Palace (where the queen ruled and where she was later dethroned and imprisoned) and the state capitol.

4
Ka Huakaʻi ʻEhā

Bernice Pauahi Bishop Museum Planetarium (A)
and
Hawaiian Canoe Paddling (B)

A.

At Bishop Museum Planetarium you will experience the "Monument to the Stars—A Study of Ancient Cultures and the Sky" show. This presentation demonstrates how different people over the ages have used information contained in the skies in their everyday lives. Explore topics from early Polynesian voyages, Egyptian pyramids, the ruins of Mexican cities and Stonehenge to the modern observatories on Mauna Kea on the island of Hawaiʻi.

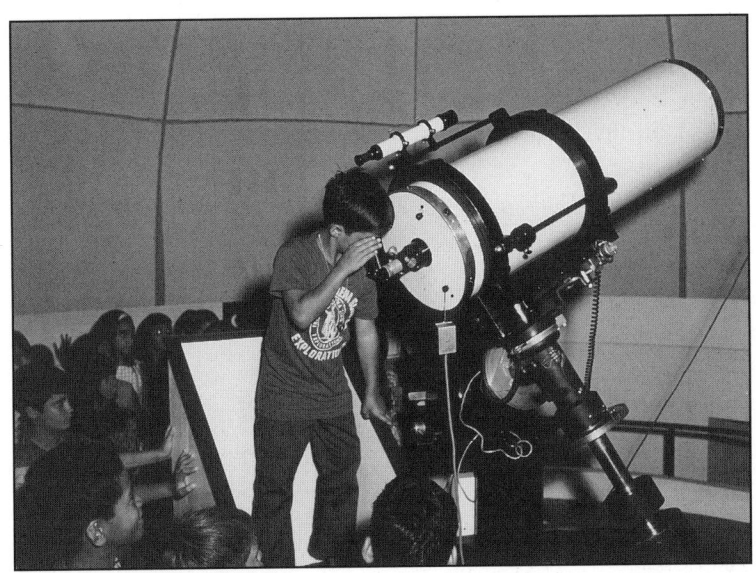

B.

Ka poʻe kahiko (the people of old), our Hawaiian ancestors, traveled across the open ocean in search of a new home, later to be called Hawaiʻi. They were strong and understood the natural elements surrounding them. They respected the *noʻeau* (wisdom) and *moʻolelo* (history) passed down over generations. These beliefs they carried with them to their new home.

This *huakaʻi* (field trip) uses the *manaʻo* (thoughts) necessary to travel successfully by sea. From learning in the classroom about *lōkahi* (unity), *laulima* (working together), *paʻahana* (working hard), *mālama* (caring for others) and *hōʻihi* (respect), *ka poe mākaʻikaʻi* (the explorers) are able to practice these values while they *hoe waʻa* (paddle the canoe).

5
Ka Huaka'i 'Elima

Polynesian Cultural Center

Polynesian Cultural Center is located in Lā'ie, the *ahupua'a* (land division usually extending from the uplands to the sea) of Lā'iemalo'o. The 42-acre center features seven Pacific island villages, showcasing the ancient life-styles of Tonga, Tahiti, Fiji, the Marquesas, Sāmoa, New Zealand's Maori and Hawai'i.

We will visit the Hawaiian village. We will see some of the plants which were here when the first Hawaiians came—such as *milo, hau, 'ilima* and *hāpu'u*. We will also see those introduced by the ancient Polynesians—such as *kī, kō, mai'a, hala, 'ulu, niu* and *kalo*. At the village one may see how *kalo* is grown and made into *poi*.

In the village we will also see plants introduced by later foreigners—such as ginger and the calabash tree. Hawaiians invented uses for some of these plants and today they are still used for cultural purposes.

Home Hoʻonaʻauao
Boarding Life

As students of Hoʻomākaʻikaʻi you are brought to the Kamehameha Schools campus to live in dormitories for one week. Life on the Kamehameha Schools campus is a time to share, to give, to meet new friends and, most of all, to have fun.

You will experience such shared values of the *ʻohana* (extended family) setting as: *laulima* (cooperation), *kuleana* (responsibility), *ʻike* (recognition) and *kōkua* (helping one another). These values will become a part of your daily activities.

From these values you will better understand the heritage of which you may be justly proud. With this year's theme of *"hoʻokūpono"* your experiences of these values will be an important and continuing part of your life. These experiences will confirm your sense of *lōkahi* (unity and harmony). It is an opportunity to enrich yourself and open wide the doors to self-fulfillment.

Dorm Life

Names of Our Dormitory *Hui*

ikaika (strong)
maka'ala (alert)

'onipa'a (firm)
ha'aheo (proud)

hanohano (honorable)
kūpono (honest)

kilakila (majestic)
kaulana (famous)

'eleu (energetic)
na'auao (wise)

The name of my friend is _____

Sunday

Today I learned…

Monday

157

Attach Your Postcard Here

Tuesday

If your feet could talk, what stories would they tell about your day's experiences?

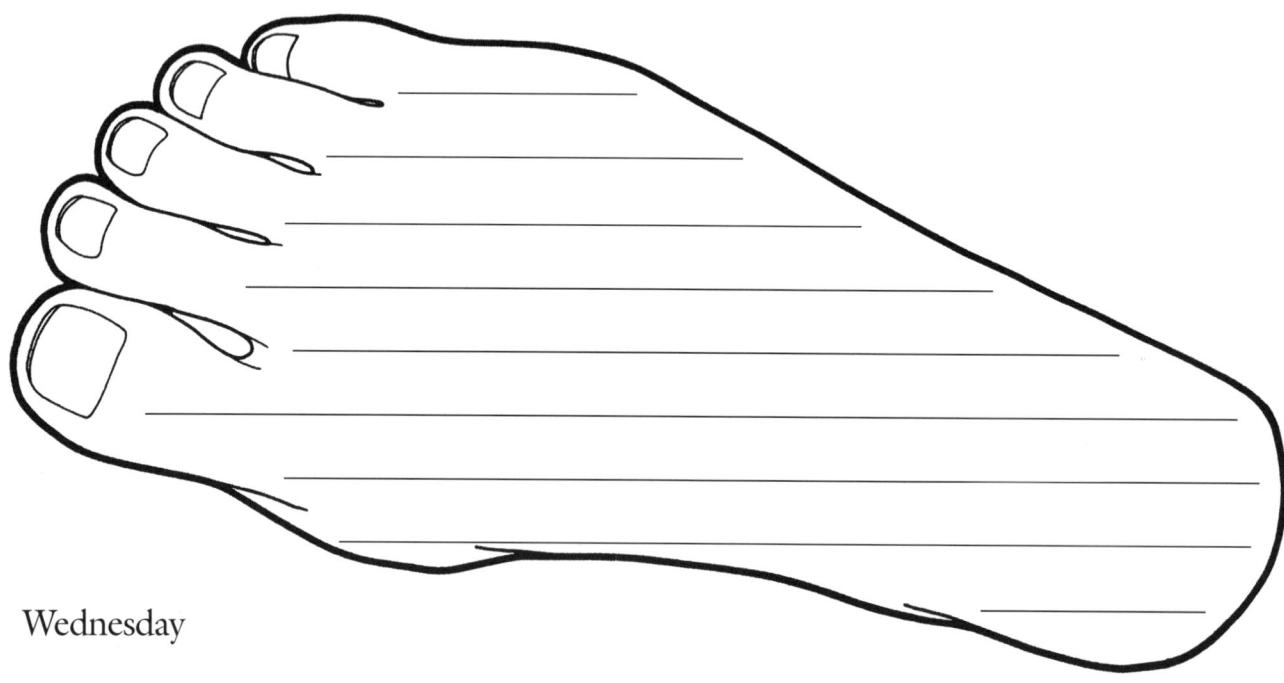

Wednesday

The thing I am going to remember about the Ho'omāka'ika'i Program is…

Thursday

Ka Palapalaʻāina O Ke Kula
campus map

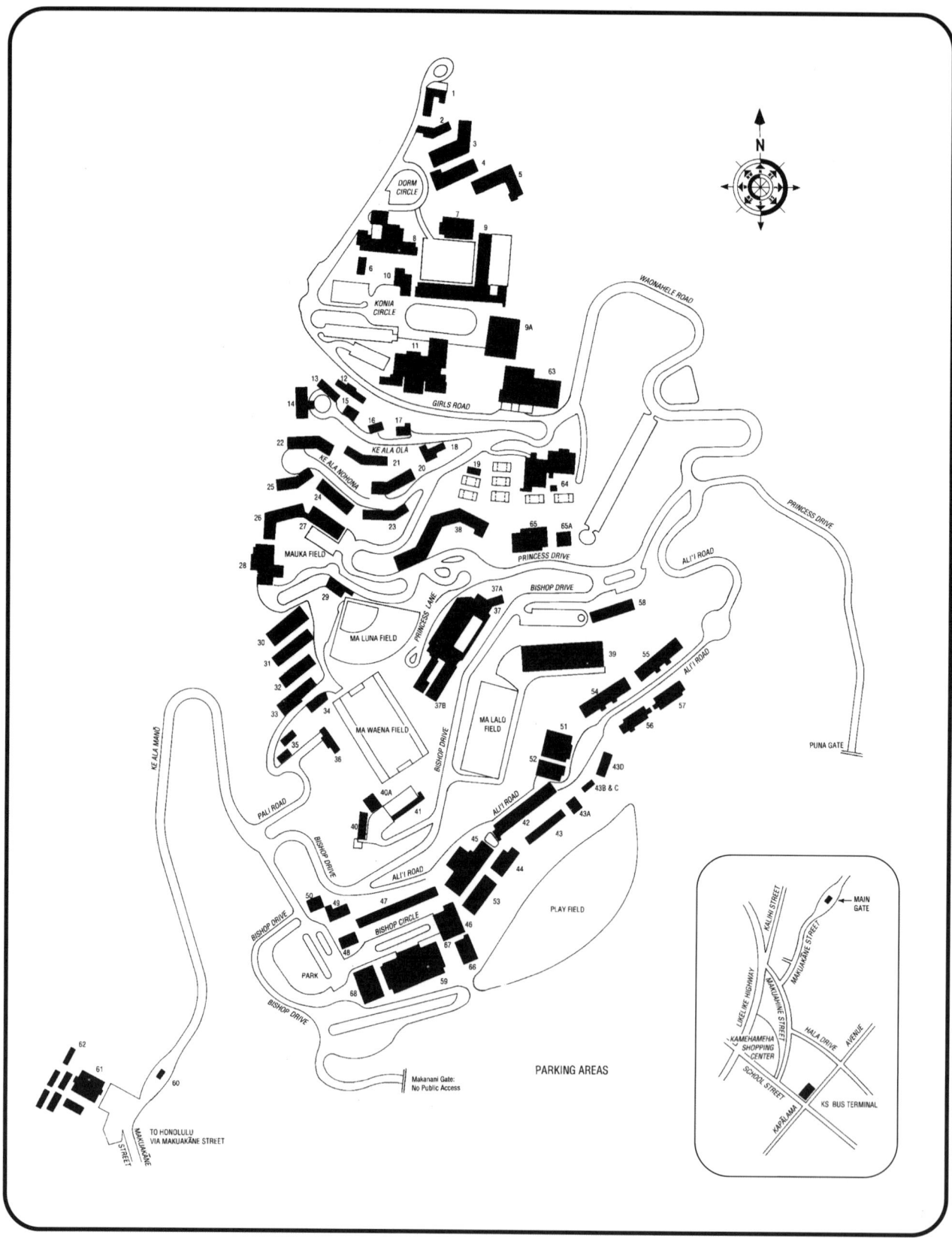

Key

1	Keōpūolani-Uka	37A	Physical Education
2	Keōpūolani-Kai	37B	Athletics
3	Kapiʻolani Nui	38	Pākī
4	Kekāuluohi	39	Kekūhaupiʻo
5	Kīnaʻu	40	Electrical/Paint/Plumbing Shops
6	Haleakalā Annex	40A	Base Yard Storage
7	Kaʻahumanu	41	Rifle Range
8	Haleakalā	42	Kaʻōleiokū
9	Konia	43	Liliʻuokalani
9A	Frank E. Midkiff Learning Center	43A	Classroom #65
10	W. O. Smith	43B	Classroom #66
11	Princess Ruth Keʻelikōlani (Performing Arts Complex)	43C	Classroom #67
		43D	Classroom #68
12	Hale Kukui	44	Keliʻimaikaʻi
13	Hale Mālama Ola	45	Kalama
14	Hale Ola	46	Kalanimōkū
15	Hale Hānai	47	Kūihelani
16	Hale Alakaʻi	48	Nāhiʻenaʻena
17	Hale Kahu	49	Kānekapōlei
18	Hale Pelekikena	50	Keolaokalani
19	Tennis Courts/Locker Rooms	51	Keawe
20	Lunalilo	52	Keawe Locker Room
21	Kapuāiwa	53	Kaiona
22	ʻIolani	54	Alice E. Knapp
23	Kamehameha	55	Maude Post
24	Liholiho	56	Kaʻiulani
25	Kaleiopapa	57	Kekūāiwa
26	Keōua	58	Princess Bernice Pauahi Adm. Bldg.
27	Bishop Hall	59	Kamāmalu
28	Kekūanaoʻa	60	Guard Station
29	Hale Koa	61	Ulupono
30	Physical Plant	62	Ulupono
31	Physical Plant/Transportation/Security	63	ʻAkahi
32	Carpenter Shop	64	Kapoukahi
33	Motor Pool/Welding Shop	65	Bernice Pauahi Bishop Memorial Chapel
34	Motor Pool	65A	Bernice Pauahi Bishop Heritage Center
35	Storage Buildings	66	Keʻeaumoku
36	Hale Mawaena A, B & C	67	Kekuʻiapoiwa
37	Pool	68	Kekelaokalani

Nā Inoa Hale
building names

names of the classrooms and dormitories	identification
ʻIolani	Name given to Kamehameha II and Kamehameha III, it means Royal Hawk.
Liholiho	Kamehameha II, eldest son of Kamehameha I and Keōpūolani. He and his queen died in London of measles.
Kapuāiwa	Kamehameha V, son of Kīnaʻu and Kekūanaoʻa.
Kamehameha	The name of the dynasty of kings founded by Kamehameha I. They ruled Hawaiʻi from 1795 to 1873.
Kaleiopapa	Kamehameha III, also known as Kauikeaouli; second son of Kamehameha I and Keōpūolani. Kalama was his queen.

Other Facilities

ʻAkahi	Aunt of Princess Bernice Pauahi Bishop, ʻAkahi left her estate to Princess Ruth.
Hale Ola	Health Center
Princess Ruth Keʻelikōlani	Cousin of Princess Pauahi, she gave Pauahi vast landholdings which form the largest part of Bishop Estate and support the Kamehameha Schools.
Kekūhaupiʻo	Noted teacher, warrior, counselor and companion to Kamehameha I.

Illustrators and Designers

Mary Carvalho Robin Yoko Burningham

Nancy Middlesworth Lynn Criss Fujita

Revised Music Notation by:

Gayla Traylor